AF539786

VOCATIONAL EDUCATION OF HEARING IMPAIRED STUDENTS

VOCATIONAL EDUCATION OF HEARING IMPAIRED STUDENTS

By

Dr. S. VIJAYA VARDHINI

Assistant Professor
Department of Education & HRD
Dravidian University
KUPPAM – 517 462
Chittoor (A.P.)

DISCOVERY PUBLISHING HOUSE PVT. LTD.
NEW DELHI-110 002

First Published – 2010
Reprinted – 2017

ISBN: 978-81-8356-609-4

Vocational Education of Hearing Impaired Students

Published by:
DISCOVERY PUBLISHING HOUSE PVT. LTD.
4383/4B, Ansari Road Darya Ganj
New Delhi - 110 002 (India)
Phone: +91-11-23279245, 43596064-65
Fax: +91-11-23253475
E-mail: discoverypublishinghouse@gmail.com
sales@discoverypublishinggroup.com
web: www.discoverypublishinggroup.com

Printed at:
Infinity Imaging Systems
Delhi

PREFACE

In ancient times the disabled were often discarded or destroyed from the society, they felt that they were unfit and a burden to the society. As per NSSO survey 2002, the number of disabled persons in our country was 1.85 crore and 1.8% of the total population. Among them 9% of deaf were in urban area and 10% in rural area. The major problem of the deaf or hard of hearing Person is with communication, backwardness in language, speech and in vocabulary leads to inability to comprehend the meaning, concept, abstract feelings and complex structure of languages.

In today's competitive world it goes without saying that one has to strive hard to prove his capability to grab the opportunities in the society. When it is difficult for a person with all the organs and senses intact to achieve financial stability, it is even more difficult for a handicapped like deaf. They have the prominent drawback of communication lag.

The vocational education will build the self-esteem of the deaf individuals, and helps them to develop their ability to work and live independently. In case of the disabled, vocational education and rehabilitation become more essential. Unless the system of education increases the levels of confidence in them, they cannot come of the diffidence. Hence, they should be provided with vocational education to meet the future challenges.

The book consists of two sections. In the first section, I focussed my attention on the aims of Education, Vocational Education with respect to various Committees and Commissions; Concept of Special Education, and the need of Vocational Education of Hearing Impaired children to face the challenges of future life. The available review of related literature on Vocational Education particularly in case of General Education and Special Education is furnished.

The second section focuses on the methodology, sampling, tools used, finalisation of tool, data collection, analysis and interpretation of the collected data and findings of the study, suggestion, educational implications and conclusions.

S. VIJAYA VARDHINI

ACKNOWLEDGEMENTS

I wish to express my sincere thanks to my research supervisor Prof. Ch. Vijaya Lakshmi, Professor, Department of Education, Sri Padmavati Mahila Visvavidyalayam, Tirupati, Prof. R. Venkateswara Rao, former Principal of IASE, Sri Padmavati Mahila Visvavidyalayam, Tirupati, Dr. T.G. Amutha Valli, Asstt. Professor, Deptt. of Education, Sri Padmavathi Mahila Visvavidyalayam, Tirupati and Mr. S. Mahammad Ali, Lecturer in Education, Sri Sarada College of Education, Mahaboobnagar, for their kind co-operation and timely suggestion during the tenure of research work.

I express my immense gratitude to the authorities of various special schools for the deaf who extended their full co-operation in collecting the required data for this research work.

My special thanks to my better half Sri Y.V. Sampath Kumar, Parents, all my family members and well-wishers for their co-operation in fulfilling this endeavour.

S. VIJAYA VARDHINI

CONTENTS

SECTION - I

CHAPTER 1

COMMITTEES AND COMMISSIONS ON VOCATIONAL EDUCATION

Education is the process in which an individual is helped to get adjusted to the changing world. The best education is one which guides the child to live his life richly and abundantly, at the same time to contribute to social betterment. The aim of education varies from race to race and generation to generation, but the emphasis has always been on the mental and psychical growth of the individual. The methods employed at various ages may also be different but the basic factor remains the same. The child is subjected to certain experiences that are intended to modify its behaviour for proper adjustment to a changing social environment.

The Indian Education Commission (1964-66) observes that:

"education must serve as a 'powerful instrument of social, economic, and cultural transformation necessary for the realization of the national goals".

The term education is a comprehensive one. It does not merely mean the acquisition of knowledge or experience but it means the development of habits, attitudes and skills which help an individual to lead a fuller and worthwhile life.

Whatever be the connotation of the term 'education', the purpose of education has been stated at different levels - general and specific forms. The purpose of general form of education is often termed as aim and the very specific purpose of it is explained as an objective.

AIMS OF EDUCATION

Aims are related to situations of life. Any system of education must meet the real situations of the community. It must be in accordance with the physical and social needs of the community. The child is a member of the community in which he lives and education must help him to become a useful member of the society. Changes in the ideals and values accepted by society are being reflected in the corresponding changes in the system of education.

The purpose of education i.e. aims of education have been categorized and stated depending on the specific and significant views of educationists and academics, which are enumerated below. It would not be out of context to enumerate some of significant aims of education in the following

Individual Aim of Education

The supporters of the individual aim of education believe that "Social institutions exist only to make the individual life better, fuller, richer, happier, more secure and therefore more fruitful than would otherwise be possible". Rousseau in his 'Social Contract' writes:

> "Man is born free; and everywhere he is in chains. One thinks he is the master of others, and still remains a greater slave than they."
>
> According to Nunn:
>
> "The education that aims at fostering individuality is the only education according to nature. As such-Education must secure conditions under which individuality is most completely developed".

The individual aim of education explains the principle of self realization of the individual.

But in fact, the individual aim of education does not deny or minimize the responsibility of man to his fellows, for individual life cannot be developed only in terms of his own nature and that is, social as truly as self regarding.

Social Aim of Education

The supporters of the social aim of education claim that the state has absolute control over the lives and destinies of the individuals living in it. According to them, society has a natural origin in human nature. So individuals cannot live outside the society. They are not only rational but also social and political beings. Here state is elevated to the pinnacle of importance. So education provides means for the students not for self realization and self expression, but for self-sacrifice for the glory of the state. Students learn to show unquestionable loyalty to the state authority. Educational progress is considered as social rather than individual.

Moral Aim of Education

According to a section of philosophers "Highest love for man may be called morality". Therefore, man is considered as a moral being and his education insists the cultivation of socially approved behaviour, "Character is the inner consistency and unity which gives steadfastness and dependability to man's conduct." Education for character building aims at conquest of higher intelligence over the lower impulses. This is otherwise called as morality. Moral qualities like justice, sincerity, honesty, tolerance, self-control etc make an individual, perfect and a human being in real spirit.

Citizenship Aim of Education

With the development of democracy, training for citizenship is advocated as the aim of education. Education should make a person a good citizen in a democratic state this view is, in fact, an outcome of Sociological approach to education. In a democratic society the political role to be played by an individual is very complicated and at the same time important. Education for citizenship should train a person to discharge his duties and make him conscious of his rights.

Knowledge Aim of Education

The study of realities, values and other information obtained through various means is known as knowledge. According to Socrates:

> "Knowledge is powerful and through it only every activity is conducted.' Shakespeare opines that "ignorance is the curse of god and knowledge is the wing which makes us to reach the heaven!"

Knowledge gives a separate entity for man and it actually separates a human being from an animal. In fact, it is a great wealth to mankind. It makes a person face any challenge in life. Though it is an important aim, it should not be the sole aim of education. It must be one to be achieved like other aims of education. In the present society, our general educational system is facing a crisis because of the excessive importance given to the knowledge aim of education. The mighty unemployment problem that exists in the society proves that mere possession of knowledge is not a guarantee for an employment or the settlement in life. It must be clubbed with other aims of education.

Vocational Aim of Education

If specific training is given to an individual in a specific vocation in order to seek out his livelihood in future, that kind of education is called vocationalization of education. This aim is an ancient one. Vocational Education was given by older members of the family during ancient days and it was transmitted hereditarily from one generation to another. In addition, the children can have an added advantage of living in the same environment and learn the skills of the vocation very easily and effectively. Besides, he need not go in search of employment in his adult life. This kind of education has utilitarian value. All modem societies are marching towards this aim. For the children of low intelligence it is of immense use and best suited. But this sort of education makes a person mechanical but not creative.

According to Emerson:

> "Education should be one part words, one part worship and one part work". It is education that can tame the animal in the man. It can also train the man as a toolmaker and tool user. For this he needs the information, instruction, inspiration and also education for vocation".

EDUCATION FROM THE VIEW POINT OF PHILOSOPHERS

Ancient Indian Philosophers

It appears that in ancient India, vocational education though it was not an integral part of general education was emphasised through the practice of different types of physical activities in *âshramas* by gurus. In ancient Indian society, youngsters used to learn certain skills such as hunting, generating the fire etc from their parents as apprentice. Some of the prominent views of ancient India on vocational education are as follows:

> The *Rig-Veda* says, "Education is that which makes a man self reliant and selfless". Education in the *Upanishads* is something which liberates men from all bondages. The *Bhagavad-Gita* says "Knowledge of the soul and the Brahman is Education". It actually emphasises selfless action. Yagnavalkya envisages that education makes one a man of good character and useful to the world. According to Panini 'education is training obtained from the Nature'. In view of the Kautilya 'education means training for the country and for the nation', whereas Adishankharacharya says that 'education is the realization of self'.

Modern Indian Thinkers

According to Swami Vivekananda 'education must confirm the taste, temperament, capacity of each and every student'. He emphasized that 'the end of all education, all training should be man-making'. He also believed in the education of whole man.

Sri Aurobindo the exponent of Integral education said that 'education help the growing soul draw out which is in itself'. He emphasised that 'the education should have physical, vital, mental, physical and spiritual dimensions as its integral components'.

According to Lala Lajpati Rai:

> "The aim of education is to make one profitable member of the community and not the parasite, a citizen and not an Anarchist".

He also said:

> "education should draw out of a man all that is best, most useful in him so that it may be employed to the advantage of the community and of himself as a member of the community."

The poet-laureate Ravindranath Tagore felt that the content of education should include art, music, picture-making, crafts, dramatic and dancing. He says:

> "hard work, music and art are the spontaneous overflow of our deep nature and spiritual significance".

He also said that education should be intertwined with life and society. According to him:

> "there are three sources of knowledge; Nature, Life and Teacher. Further, he is an exponent of 'Art in Craft', which one can observe in his Shantiniketan".

Mahatma Gandhi's contribution to the field of education is really outstanding. He emphasized the craft centred education. He made a stress on productivity, increasing the earning capacity of the individual and making education self-supporting. Learning is intended to be accomplished through self-experience. It is meant to couple theoretical knowledge with practical skills. He believed in the dictum of 'Craft in Art'.

Western Philosphers

According to Froebel, "Education is enfoldment of what is already unfolded in the germ. He also said that:

> "education is the development of all those capacities in the individual which will enable him to control his environment and fulfil his possibilities".

> Herbert Spencer opined that:

> education is the natural development of the child which enables him to lead a complete life. In his point of view a complete life includes:

(i) Healthy living i.e. preservation of Self Help Groups.

(ii) Vocational Training and other practical arts.

(iii) Preparation for family life, begetting and rearing of children.

(iv) Worthy citizenship.

(v) Worthy usage of leisure time.

John Dewey is the only thinker who has constructed a philosophy of education comparable in its scope and depth to that of Plato. While Plato's education philosophy rests upon his belief aristocracy and its power pure reason, Dewey's educational philosophy upon his belief in democracy and its power of scientific method. A democratic society according to Dewy is one which makes provision for participation in its good of all its members and its equal terms which success flexible readjustment of its institutions through interaction of the different forms of associated life. Dewy thought his pragmatic philosophy and the educational ideas that he practical in his model school-centred around the experience, which one will gain out of undertaking an activity. This process will result in the production of the goods and ends in the material growth.

From ancient Indian times to modern times, from western thinkers to modern Indian thinkers and Philosophers, all in an agreement showed that education is not merely acquisition of knowledge but it is making man self-reliant, selfless, useful to the community, bringing best out of the child, prepare him for vocational training and make him a worthy citizen.

RECOMMENDATIONS OF EDUCATIONAL COMMISSIONS ON VOCATIONAL EDUCATION

Various committees and commissions, pre- and post-Independence, emphasized the importance and introduction of Vocational Education in Educational Institutions.

1. Pre-independence

- **Wood's Despatch (1854):** Wood's Despatch paid attention to Vocational Education, suggested that schools and Colleges should be set up at suitable places for vocational education so that people may get ample opportunities for vocational education.

  Indian Education Commission (1882): (Hunter Commission) recommended introduction of practical subjects in secondary schools. It criticised the bookish, narrow, theoretical and impractical character of Indian Education. It felt that education must prepare the children for future life and help them to select a practical vocation. It also recommended providing some instruction in technical and industrial arts to the students.

- **Sadler's Commission (1917):** It has given importance for vocational courses, and made recommendations with regard to the introduction of technological, professional and vocational courses.

- **Hartog Committee Report (1929):** This committee suggested for the establishment of technological and occupational institutions and provision for technological and industrial education in the Universities as well.

- **Sapru Committee (1934):** The committee recommended that vocational courses in secondary schools should be provided along with general education course for solving the problems of unemployment among the educated youth.
- **Wood Abbot Report (1936):** Recommend that vocational education is in no way be considered inferior to the general education and it should be treated on par with general education. Students who complete their courses in vocational school should be awarded with school leaving certificates. Separate institution should be established for vocational education.
- **Wardha Conference (1937):** In Wardha conference under the presidentship of Mahathma Gandhi some resolutions were passed with regard to general education and vocational education. Education should centre round some form of manual and productive work and all other activities to be trained, should be as far as possible integrally related to the central handicraft with due regard to the environment of the child.
- **Zakir Husain Committee (1938):** The first and second report of this committee dealt with important handicrafts like spinning, agriculture, metal works, wood crafts and other basic handicrafts which should be introduced in the education.
- **Sargent Report (1944):** For the first time Sargent report drew the attention of the Government towards the education of the disabled or handicapped. Sargent report laid a good deal of stress on industrial and vocational education. It suggested for the full time and part time institutions in order to fulfil the requirements of all the different categories of the skilled. The Sargent report specially mentioned about the special institutions to be started for the education of the students with special needs. The special children may engage themselves in productive activities, which will be useful to them in their future life.

1. Post Independence

- **Radhakrishnan Commssion (1948):** The commission felt that at Higher Education level a large number of intermediate colleges should be opened for regular students to vocations at the end of the class X or XII. The aim of these colleges is to meet a variety of needs by giving a vocational basis to their courses and at the same time, retaining their value in a system of general education as a preparation for the university course.
- **Mudaliar Commission (1953):** Secondary Education Commission (1953) made some recommendations for the improvement of vocational capability and Efficiency. In all the secondary schools proper emphasis should be laid on crafts and productive work, and introduce various vocational courses at secondary level and provide opportunity to the students to take up agriculture or some other technical or commercial course to add something to the productive capabilities of the country.
- **Vocational Education Act of 1964:** Under public law 88-210, the Vocational Education Act of 1963 provided priority of allotments of state funds for Vocational Education Programmes for the handicapped. Under 20 USCS Section 2310, for each fiscal year, at least 10% of each state allotment under section 103 (20 USCS Section 2303) from appropriations made under section 102(a) [(20 USCS, Section 2303(a)] shall be used to pay up to 50% of the cost of programs, services and activities under sub-part 2 (20 USCS, Section 2330 et. sq.) and of program improvement and support services under subpart 3 (20 USCS, Section et. sq.) for handicapped persons.
- **Kothari Commission/National Education Commission (1964-66):** The Commission recommended that education should be related to productivity. It could be done through inculcating the value of dignity of manual labour, promotion of scientific research and technology, creating

work ethics in the society as a whole, vocationalization of secondary education, job-training for workers and promotion of education for agriculture and industry.

❖ **National Policy on Education (1968):** It recommended for equalization of educational opportunities in Vocational education. Educational facilities for the physically and mentally handicapped children should be expanded and attempts should be made to develop integrated programmes to enable the handicapped children to study in regular schools.

The NPE (1964) also emphasised the need to increase facilities or technical and vocational education. Provision of facilities for secondary and vocational education should conform broadly to the requirements of developing economy and real employment opportunities. Technical and Vocational education facilities should be appropriately diversified to cover large number of fields such as agriculture, industry, trade and commerce, medicine and public health, home management, arts and crafts, secretarial training etc.

This Commission was the first to suggest that the education of handicapped children has to be organized not merely on humanitarian grounds, but on grounds of utility. Proper education would enable the handicapped children to overcome their disability and make them useful citizens to the society. It also recommended that the constitutional directive on compulsory education should include handicapped persons as well.

❖ **Vocational Rehabilitation Act of 1973:** Section 504 which is commonly called as the Rehabilitation Act, frequently cited as an important precursor to the passage of PL 94-142. Among the other things it protects the rights of handicapped children and precludes discrimination in unemployment and educational opportunities of special children.

- **The Iswarbhai Patel Committee (1977):** The Committee pointed out that "Work experience which was intended to be an integral feature of the curriculum, at all stages, did not find a proper place in the teaching learning process that followed in introduction of the new Pattern." It defined socially useful productive work as 'Purposeful and meaningful manual work resulting in either goods or services, which are useful to the community.

- **Malkam Adiseshaiah Report or Plus 2 National Review Committee (1978):** The major recommendations of the report are work-based learning, that is, either through socially useful productive work or through the vocationalized courses. The vocational courses should be in agricultural and related rural occupational areas and in managerial, commercial, health and para-medical vocations but not in the manufacturing and engineering occupations. There should be no rigid starting of courses into the general education and vocationalized educational spectrums. Regular teachers should be appointed for vocational courses and part-time teachers may also be appointed wherever necessary. The report also recommended the extension of apprenticeship facilities to all the students who complete education in vocational streams.

- **National Policy on Education (1986):** This policy **(NPE-1986)** laid a great stress on vocationalization of higher secondary education to make education more meaningful and socially useful productive. The 10+2+3 system in the school provided for 10 years of general education is followed by a +2 stage of academic and vocational streams. This policy emphasized the need for vocationally trained teachers, adequate provision of funds, good library and laboratory facilities. Self-employment opportunities should be provided. It also said that vocational courses should not be limited to engineering and technical vocations, but these should include agriculture, business, commerce, health and para-medical services, home science etc.

- **Acharya Ramamurthi Committee (1990):** The Committee recommended that socially useful productive work should be linked with various subjects both at the level of content and pedagogy. Flexibility should be there for children to opt for different combinations of academic and vocational subjects.
- **Nedurumalli Janardhana Reddy Committee (1992):** This committee stated that work experience programme should be systematically implemented by allocation of 12.5 per cent to 20 percent of the school time for these activities leaving practical orientation in relation to the various subjects offered.

All National thinkers and educational champions from pre-independence to post-independence and from Mahatma Gandhi in late thirties to Janardhan Reddy in nineties have emphasized work education to form an important and integral component of school education.

CHAPTER 2

SPECIAL EDUCATION
HEARING IMPAIRED CHILDREN

Special Education is a branch of education, designed to study and meet the unique needs of the students with problems or special talents in thinking, seeing, hearing, speaking and socializing. In other words special education includes individual planning and systematic monitoring, arrangement of physical settings, special equipment and materials, teaching procedures and other interventions designed to help the exceptional children to achieve the greatest possible personal self-sufficiency and academic success.

To describe these exceptional children, several terms have been used subnormal or abnormal, handicapped, disabled, special, exceptional, impaired and challenged etc.

SOME DEFINITIONS

- The exceptional child was defined by the famous special educationist Krit (1962) as "The child who deviates from the average or normal child in mental, physical or social characteristics to such an extent that he/she requires a modification of school practices, special educational services in order to the maximum capacity."

- **Smith and Neisworth** (1975) defined Special Education as "the profession concerned with the arrangement or educational variable leading to the prevention, reduction or elimination of those conditions that produce significant defects in the academic, communication, Loco motor of adjustive functioning of children."
- **The World Health Organization** (1976) has clearly distinguished those terms and categorized them into three. They are Handicap, Disability and Impairment.
- **Panda** (1977) defines "Children are considered exceptional when they have some characteristics which deviate from the normal or average child."
- **Jangira** (1986) states that special education is that component of education which employs special instructional methodology, instructional material, competencies to meet educational needs of persons with specific disabilities.
- **UNESCO's** (1987) International classification of special education is specially designed for exceptional students who may be retarded, learning disabled, emotionally disturbed, Deaf or hard of hearing, visually impaired or physically handicapped or gifted.

From the above definitions it can be said that special education includes all aspects of education which apply to the exceptional children.

The special children are those who deviate significantly from the normal ones, i.e. they differ physically, mentally, emotionally and socially and are mainly classified into four:

1. Gifted
2. Mentally Retarded

3. Physically Handicapped such as blind, deaf, orthopaedically handicapped etc.
4. Socially handicapped such as orphans, destitute etc.

THE PHYSICALLY HANDICAPPED

A person who is affected with a physical impairment which limits his/her participation in any normal activity is called as physically handicapped. The physically handicapped include the deaf i.e., partially deaf or hard of hearing, blind, crippled, cerebral palsied etc. The present study, concentrates only on the hearing impaired.

HEARING IMPAIRMENT—CLASSIFICATION

Based on the level of Degree of Hearing Loss they are classified as:

1. Mild (20-40 dB);
2. Moderate (40-50dB);
3. Severe (60-75 dB); and
4. Profound (75 dB & above).

The conference of executives of American schools (Kirk 1970) made a classification with regard to hearing handicapped children to avoid confusion in terminology, i.e.

> **The Deaf**: "The deaf are those in whom the sense of hearing is non functional for the ordinary purpose of life." Or The total inability to hear is also called as Deaf or deafness.
>
> **The Hard of hearing**: Those in whom the sense of hearing although defective is functional with or without hearing aid.

PROBLEMS OF HEARING IMPAIRED

1. The major problem of the deaf or hard of hearing person is with communication. Backwardness in language, speech and in vocabulary leads to inability to comprehend the meaning, concept, abstract feelings and complex structure of languages.

2. The poor self-concept which is significant in them damages the development of their personality.
3. The deaf children have a big problem in understanding the abstract concepts. It is because of limited vocabulary and poor comprehension ability.
4. In vocational adjustment they are facing many difficulties i.e. formal or Non-formal education in any field requires minimum language to be qualified. Now-a-days all the vocations are dependent on one qualification or the other. Even though the minimum level to pass a course is reduced to suit their disability, in the vocational arena they face difficulty to compute with the hearing folk. So pre-vocational training and vocational education will help them to settle comfortably in a vocation.

HEARING IMPAIRED: A HISTORICAL VIEW

International Scenario

The hearing impaired children have been the victims of social negligence through history. They were hated, ignored and socially boycotted till recent past, but now a change has occurred in the attitude of the people towards these deaf children. It may be due to the awareness of the problems faced by disabled people or political system which provides equal educational opportunities for all without any discrimination of caste, creed and sex or any other like handicapped.

In ancient times the disabled were often discarded or destroyed from the society, they felt that they were unfit and a burden to the society. The ancient Greeks used to exterminate the handicapped among them, on the principle that "Only the fit have the right to survive."

In the middle ages the handicapped or differently abled, disabled children were exploited and were used for amusement purpose.

Ponce De Leon (1520-1584) is generally considered to be the first teacher of the deaf who established a school for the deaf in Spain. Initially he started with writing and progressed to speech. Thus, Spain was the first to introduce systematic language teaching for deaf children. He used oral communication and structural approach for language development. Ponce de Leon was followed by Pablo Bonnet (1579-1620). Bonnet used a method which proceeded from finger spelling to the articulation of sounds, syllabus and word for reading and writing. Dalgarno (1626-87) was the first to use finger spelled alphabet to teach deaf children. He used natural approach in teaching language to the hearing impaired.

Hohn Wallance (1616-1703), William Holder (1616-98), John Kanard Amman (1669-1724) and Henny Baker (1698-1774), were the pioneers in oral methods of teaching the deaf.

Samuel Heinicke was called as the father of German methods of teaching the Deaf and contributed for the establishment of first public school in Germany. The other noteworthy contributors were Abbe Stork, Calnde Francis abbe Deschemps, Loreno Hervas of Parduo, JFL Arnold, Henry Deniel Guyot, and Thoman Braidwood etc.

Charles Michel Del Epee (1712-1789) and Samuel Heinicke are highly praiseworthy for the establishment of the first two state supported public schools for deaf in the world - one at pairs and the other in England. Wheave An Del Dpee Nar called as "Father of the signs" successfully used the signs method in teaching deaf. He developed and published the first dictionary and grammar of signs. With the growing awareness of educating the deaf, emerging in European countries, people of other countries also slowly realized the need and capability of educating deaf. Until second decade of 19th century no intensive efforts had taken place in educating the deaf children in the United States. The first permanent school for deaf students, in U.S.A., was established by Thoman Hopkins Gallaudet in 1817. With the efforts of Rev John in 1818 another permanent school for the deaf was established. In 1818 the New York Institution was established in Washington D.C. for the instruction of Deaf and Dumb. This school has essentially developed as a college and later it became a university unit and was renamed as Gallaudet University. A Central Institute of Deaf was founded in 1914 at St. Louis with the objectives of training, service and research in the field of Deaf Education.

The formation of American Association for the Deaf in 1890 was another important landmark in American history of Deaf Education. This was to promote speed reading and residual hearing in deaf.

The 20th century witnessed a series of rapid advancements in the field of Deaf Education. Achievement in Science and Technology helped in developing sophisticated devices including appliances, techniques and methods which aimed at improving the quality of deaf education. The development took place in western countries immigrated to the other parts of the world thereby promoting the universalized status of the deaf education.

National Scenario

In ancient Indian literature we can find that disabled persons were treated with great compassion and a large portion of the state income was set aside for the maintenance of the handicapped persons during the reign of the great emperors like Ashoka and Harsha.

During the period of Marathas the deaf people were sometimes used as spies and even confidential correspondence was also made by them. It shows that the hearing impairers were treated as useful citizens of the society in those times, though there was no mention about the deaf people being educated in any school.

In the olden days where the deaf were considered as uneducable, and lived on the mercy, were taken care of by the family members in the Joint Family System. In 1884 the first attempt to educate the deaf was started at Mazagaon in Bombay presidency by a Roman Catholic Mission, and in 1885 the first school for the deaf was started. Bengal was the second State to take the lead in this direction. In 1893 the Calcutta Deaf and Dumb School was established in the eastern zone. In 1896 the third institute for the deaf came into existence in Palayamokottia in the southern parts of India. Subsequently Deaf Education made progress in other States of India. In 1908, a school for the deaf muter was established at Allahabad, in 1909 Muku Vidyalayam at Boroda. In 1911 Barisil Deaf and Dumb School in Bengal, in 1912 C.S.I. School for the Deaf at Madras, in 1913 School for the Deaf and Blind at Mehsana, in Bhonsle Deaf and Dump School at Nagapur, in 1916 Dacced Deaf and Dumb School in Bengal, in 1926 Little Flower Convent School for the Deaf at Madras and in 1931 Government Lady Noyce School for the Deaf in Delhi were started respectively.

There were 38 schools for the deaf by the time India became independent, as quoted by Kundu (2000).

The convention of the teachers of the deaf in 1935 was a landmark in the history of the education of the deaf in India. In that convention they urged the Government

(i) Compulsory and free education for the deaf;

(ii) To create awareness in the public towards education of the deaf;

(iii) To establish more schools for the deaf;

(iv) To provide facilities for research in the field of education for the deaf; and

(v) To provide facilities for organised teaching.

The International Year of the Disabled Persons (IYDP) plan of action

Indian IYDP was formally inaugurated on 5th January 1981. This paved the way for the establishment of Ali Yavar Jung National Institute for Hearing Handicapped (AYJNIHH) at

Bombay in 1983. Quite a number of important activities were undertaken during the period such as awareness campaigns, and a new scheme of financial assistance for purchase of aids and appliances was framed. It was also decided to start three more special employment exchanges for the handicapped, eleven rural rehabilitation centres, special roaster point for effective implementation and reservation quota in education as well as in employment.

National Policy on Education (1986)

Objectives of this policy include, the integration of the disabled with the general community as equal partners, to prepare them for normal growth and enable them to face life with courage and confidence, to start vocational training for the disabled with adequate arrangements, proposed reorientation of teacher training programmes for teachers on how to deal with special children.

Programme of Action (1992)

The National Policy on Education (1986) was followed by this programme of Action (1992) with the establishment and expansion of special schools, integrated programmes, vocational training centres etc.

As per NSSO survey 2002, the number of disabled persons in our country was 1.85 crore and 1.8% of the total population. Among them 9% of Deaf were in urban areas and 10% in rural areas.

CONSTITUTIONAL PROVISIONS

The Indian Constitution guarantees that disabled people should have the same rights as other normal members of the society. In the Directive Principles of the Indian Constitution Article 38 emphasized that State should promote the welfare of all the people including disabled. Article 39 ensures that all citizens have the right to have an adequate means of livelihood. Article 41 affirms security and human conditions to work.

Article 43 emphasizes on securing to all workers a living wage, ensuring a decent standard of life, full enjoyment of leisure, social and cultural opportunities. Article 45 assures free and compulsory education to all children, till the age of 14 years.

The significance of vocational education and its relevance to Indian life was realised even in pre-independent India and it received increased attention in post independence era and also in Indian constitutional provisions. A re-look into the origin and development of the concept of vocational education in India and the programme of action initiated by the government from time to time would only reveal the prominent place of vocational education which has been receiving in our national plans.

EDUCATION FOR VOCATION

The primary needs of man are food, shelter and clothing. If education does not make the child to procure these three all the other ideas of education become meaningless and irrelevant. No one can deny the significance of economic needs of man. They must make person worthy and a contributing citizen to his country. Civic efficiency comes up through economic independence only. Therefore education must prepare the child to take up for some profession or vocation in his future.

Education must train the child to lead a responsible living. The knowledge that the child has gained in the school will be of no use, if he/she cannot have on economically independent life. That means the knowledge that the child acquired in the school must become an instrument in earning a decent income in his/her later life. Therefore vocational bias in education is very essential. The importance in vocational bias has been recognised in the basic education system, which is work-centred or craft-centred.

The vocational education in the most efficient manner helps the hearing challenged individuals for their planning and career development concern. The vocational education will build the self esteem of the deaf individuals, and helps them to develop their ability to work and live independently.

Concept of Vocational Education

The term 'vocational education' is a comprehensible one. Vocational education is the education for manual work. This concept centres on the idea of ability to work with hands rather than mind with a curriculum of certain manual activities like leather work, wood work, metal work, drawing etc.

It is an Organized Educational Programme which directly related to the preparation of individual for paid or unpaid employment, or for additional preparation for a career requirement.

The goal of vocational education programme is to prepare the students to enter the world of work and to develop the basic academic skills, good work habits, meaningful work values, skills, aptitudes, occupational opportunities, the ability to plan and to make career decisions and securing employment. The basic components of vocational education are specific job training information, personal and social adjustment skills, career information and modified content in subject areas. Occupational activities which we can find in vocational programmes are paid work experience during the day, paid work experience after school hours, and unpaid work observation as in-school vocational laboratory (classroom).

Vocational education is that which is Craft-oriented. The major objective of Craft-oriented education is to aid the learners to acquire the greatest work efficiency possible in earning their living by providing special instruction in a single craft or trade. This is for productive purposes or socially useful productive work. It aims at training the workers in their specified area.

Vocational education is the education, in certain specified subjects, which may be of vocational or technical nature, generally confined to secondary stage in education. This concept implies that a specified part of the curriculum is either vocational or technical, the remaining part falling under general or liberal education coverage.

Vocational education is the education or training of workers. This concept implies that any kind of education or training in which a worker participates is vocational education.

Apart from general education vocational education indicates acquisition of knowledge and practical skills in different sectors of economic and social life. It is an integral part of general education. It prepares the individual to select a particular vocation or occupation. It gives practical orientation to education which becomes meaningful and brings utility to the education. It is not merely technical training but more than that. It prepares the individual to understand the social reality and to realise his own potential within the framework of economic development. It prepares the individual for specific competencies in different vocations.

Vocational Education for the Children with Special Needs

It is clearly evident that almost all committees and commissions on school education unequally emphasized the need for vocationalization of secondary education. This has become inevitable in the socio-economic context of our society. Though number of efforts have been made to vocationalize the secondary education skill it has not yet reached the satisfactory level of the educational planners on one hand and on the other the community at large. But still both at national and state level, number of initiatives are made to see that vocalization of secondary education becomes a successful one. This status of vocationalization of secondary education is as far as main stream of secondary education in concerned. In the light of this scenario, if one looks at the vocationalization of secondary education for the children with special needs in general and the hearing-impaired in particular, the situation is very alarming. It is rather very essential to develop certain vocational skills taking into consideration the disability of these challenged children. In view of their survival and sustenance in future society without depending upon others not only providing education to these peoples the vocationalization of education should be considered on priority.

NEED FOR THE STUDY

Providing vocational education and preparing the children with special needs in general and hearing impaired children in particular for various self-employments, an occupation has always been an important task in the total educational system. It prepares the individual to lead a better life and to attain better economic and civic amenities.

Majority of the hearing impaired students need the secondary school education with vocational training and post school training for their future employment. The hearing impaired children can successfully be employed in suitable jobs only after undergoing proper vocational training.

It is very much evident that vocational education will enable the child to get economic independence. The economic stability should improve the quality life of the hearing impaired child. A job or employment is the only answer to the hearing impaired child to progress himself as a free, independent and useful citizen to the community. The personality of a hearing impaired will totally be changed by providing suitable employment only. They can lead a secured life and feel proud of themselves. The abilities of the deaf children are to be recognised but not their disabilities.

In today's competitive world it goes without saying that one has to strive hard to prove his capability to grab the opportunities in the society. When it is difficult for a person with all the organs and senses intact to achieve financial stability, it is even more difficult for a handicapped like deaf. They have the prominent drawback of communication lag. In such cases vocational education and rehabilitation become more essential. Unless the system of education increases the levels of confidence in them, they cannot come of the diffidence. Hence they should be provided with vocational education to meet the future challenges.

Vocationalization of education has not yet taken deep roots in the country. For children with disability vocationalization of education is most important concept of socially useful productive work. It should be implemented, if necessary with some modifications in schools for the hearing impaired children.

The vocational education of hearing impaired plays a vital role in their career choice and in career education. Career education is a life cantered approach focusing on the individual on a production worker in many lives centred jobs.

Education of disabled is considered to be the prime concern and top priority should be given to their rehabilitation and employment. The Government of India aims to impart education to each and every child of the country through different programmes including children with special needs, since education is the beginning of employment; special attention is now given to the education of persons with disability.

The hearing impaired adolescents who will get vocational education at secondary level learn dignity of labour and derives pleasure from work.

More employment opportunities after good education and proper training in particular skills are very much essential for the hearing impaired children, so that they can go forward and become successful economically and self-sufficient.

Against this background it will be appropriate to evaluate the present conditions of the schools meant for hearing impaired children so that an estimate could be made whether the needed facilities are available in the schools if these are not available to what extent the conditions are to be improved. It also throws light on various vocational skills and their relevance, adequacy of technical knowledge of the teachers or the short comings and gives suggestions for improvement.

The other significant dimension would be to study the linkages of the practical skills provided through a vocation with that of the future occupations which they choose to get settled in life.

In this context it is desirable to look at the infrastructure facilities, qualified teaching staff, whether there is a passive correlation between what is expected of the schools and what is being achieved, whether the students coming out of the schools do have necessary self-confidence and self-reliance to face the challenges of future life and also to suggest ways and means to give a futuristic direction for the improvement of such schools at large.

Hence, a study of vocational education has gained importance to the hearing impaired student in specific and schools at secondary level in Andhra Pradesh was general is taken up in this work.

SCOPE OF THE STUDY

The present study was limited to the hearing impaired students who were studying in special schools for the deaf at secondary level in the age group of 12-18 years in all the three regions of Andhra Pradesh.

This study is intended to focus the attention primarily on the vocational needs of Hearing Impaired children, and the type of vocational education imparted by the special school for the hearing impaired children. In this study the investigator examined the problem from the view of students and Teachers. It did not take into account the parents' views and their socio-economic background.

CHAPTER 3

RESEARCH STUDIES ON VOCATIONAL EDUCATION FOR HEARING IMPAIRED CHILDREN

Review of Literature widens knowledge, deepens the understanding and builds up ideas and insights for better perspective and therefore it is an essential aspect of any research. In this chapter the literature is presented fewer than two headings:

1. studies related to vocational education of General/Normal students; and
2. studies related to vocational education of special/Hearing impaired students.

REVIEWS RELATED TO VOCATIONAL EDUCATION (GENERAL EDUCATION)

Gokhale, H.V. (1984) conducted a study on "A Study of Vocationalization at +2 Stages" and found that:

1. The vocational courses which are at present run are useful when compared to general courses. But these are failed to prepare the students for any job or self-employment venture;

2. The Government is not providing any job or financial assistance to the students passing out with vocational courses;
3. The practical training imparted through visits to different institutions and by arranging guest lectures is not sufficient;
4. Teachers needed to be trained on all practical aspects in their respective subjects.
5. The grants provided by the government are insufficient for imparting practical training.

Grewal, S.S. and Satish Kumar (1984) in their study on "Vocational Attitude of High School Students in Relation to their Intelligence and Adjustment" found that there was significant difference between students of rural and urban group with respect to their intelligence, adjustment. Vocational attitude got the factorial structure in urban while the rural group remained the same. The results of factor analysis both for urban and rural groups got imperial support in obtaining intelligence and adjustment and correlating of vocational attitude which was confirmed in the light of significant correlation.

Reddy, V.R. (1984) made a survey on existing vocationalization of school education in Andhra Pradesh. The major findings of the study were:

1. socially useful productive work which was conceived in schools as work-oriented educational activity was contributing towards the total development of the learners personality;
2. In the implementation of the socially useful productive work programme in schools, the problems encountered included non-availability of specialized teachers, inadequate physical and infrastructure facilities, non-supply of copies of syllabus (non-availability of funds and absence of guidelines for the disposal of finished products produced in the socially useful productive work programme).

Mohanty, G (1986) made a study on "Survey on Vocational Education of Orrissa" and found that:

1. Very few schools were imparting vocational education;
2. Men were more attracted towards vocational education rather than women;
3. Shortage of skilled persons;
4. No placement Service Wing;
5. Courses were not need-based;
6. Lack of practical experience made the students technically unfit for the job, even though they successfully complete their education.

Gogate, S.B. (1987) conducted a study on "Vocationalization of Education at Higher Secondary Stage in Andhra Pradesh, Tamil Nadu and West Bengal". The outcome of his study with reference to Andhra Pradesh was that, teachers who were teaching vocational courses were untrained and inadequate.

Martin, A. and Porus De (1987) conducted a study on "Vocational Interest of High School students". It was found that preference for occupational field was not related to father's occupation, education or income levels except for intellectual field. Student's preference for intellectual occupation was positively related to father's income.

When the level of the father's income was high, more number of students than expected got high score and when the level of the father's income was low, more number of students than expected got low scores for their interest in intellectual field.

Sugra, Chanawola (1987) made a study on "Occupational Choice of First Generation Learners". It was found that "the aspirations held by the family and the self decisions regarding occupations as well as the academic performance of the student are important determinants in occupational selection."

Rebert (1988) in his "A Study of the Socio-economic Status and Vocational choice of Students", found that:

1. Vocational choice of higher secondary students in relation to socio-economic status was independent, and the vocational aspiration of their parents was high.
2. Both Boys and Girls had similar vocational choices towards agriculture, arts, literature, executive, commerce, science and social work.

Emmanuel M.A.K.J (1990) conducted a study on "Vocationalisation of Education at +2 Stage: A Study of Some Major Problems of Vocationalisation of Education in Andhra Pradesh". He concluded that although there was a need felt for vocational courses in the state but there was neither a proper management structure to implement the scheme nor regular teaching personnel and necessary infrastructure facilities in the vocational institutions.

Gupta, V (1990) made a study on "Vocationalisation of Education at +2 in Union Territory of Delhi". He found that the management of vocational school was weak, the courses were not need-based and linkages were yet to be established.

Javed, A.K. (1990) made a critical study on the "Vocational Interests of the Students of Arts, Science and Commerce Studying at Post-Graduation Level in Senior Colleges in the Rural Areas". It was fond that the rural students were disinterested in vocations based on agriculture. They showed much interest in science-based vocations. While students of art and commerce expressed high interest in persuasive and executive vocations, students who had all facilities showed low and little interest in social vocations. They preferred and were highly interested in white-colour jobs as against vocations requiring physical labour in which they were least interested.

Mishra, K.M. (1990) conducted a study on "Vocational Interests of Secondary School Students in Relation to this Sex, Residence and socio-economic status". The findings of the study are:

1. there was no significant difference in case of scientific, business and official activities of vocational interest, where as these have significant difference in the mechanical, agricultural, social service, Art and administration area of vocational interest;
2. there was no significant residence difference in case of business, social service and official activities of interest, where as the difference in case of scientific, mechanical, Agricultural, Art and Administration one of Interest use significant.

Misra, C.K. and **Varma, A.P.** (1990) made "A Quick Appraisal of the Implementation of the Centrally Sponsored Scheme of Vocationalisation of Secondary Education".

It was found that the management system as suggested in CSS had not been fully implemented at various levels. The district vocational sources for identification of courses and institutions were not completed. There was dearth of text books, teacher's guides, practical manual and other instructional material in almost all the vocational courses. No full time teachers were appointed. The In-service teacher training programmes organised were grossly inadequate. While work sheds were constructed in 197 out of 200 institutions, a majority of them had a shortage of furniture and library books. No provision was made for raw materials and other contingencies.

Mohan, S. and Gupta, N. (1990) conducted a study on "Vocational Students Carrier Behaviour and their Adjustment in Course at +2 Stage". They found that girls in the vocational stream showed a greater sense of satisfaction with availability of vocational curricula in comparison to girls in the academic stream. While girls in the vocational stream showed a rise in career maturity, whereas boys showed a decline. The study insists on the recommendation of the boys to introduce to the vocational courses at the secondary stage rather than at senior secondary stage.

Raizada, P.L. and Sachetin (1990) made "A Quick Appraisal of the Implementation of the Centrally Sponsored Scheme of Vocationalisation of Secondary Education in Gujarat". Certain inadequacies and drawbacks in the implementation of the scheme, related to selection of institutions, management structure, district surveys, selection of courses, curriculum design, instruction materials, collaboration arrangement, student's future and utilization of available funds were discovered.

Varma (1990) made a similar study on "A Quick Appraisal of the Centrally-sponsored of Vocationalisation of Secondary Education in Delhi". The study showed that weak points in the implementation included employment of only part-time teachers, no vocational survey, inadequate vocational guidance and dearth of instructional materials on the job training and collaboration arrangements.

Vid, D.K. and Sen Gupta, M. (1990) conducted a study on "A Quick Appraisal of the Implementation of the Centrally-sponsored Scheme of Vocationalisation of Secondary Education in Goa". The study highlighted that about 11.2 per cent of all the higher secondary students had been diverted to the vocational stream. No systematic vocational survey was conducted. About 62 per cent of the Heads of Institutions felt that the practical training given to students was inadequate. About 75 percent of teachers reported inadequate instructional materials and equipment. seventy six per cent teachers had not undergone any specialized training in vocational education. No vocational guidance was provided to the students.

Bhargava, R (1991) made a study on "The Interest and Difficulties Faced by the Students Studying in Vocational Education Stream". He found the majority of the students were interested in vocational education because of its employment preparatory nature. Lack of physical facilities, non-availability of trained teachers, not release of funds in time were some of the major, short coming identified in his study.

Dhote, A.K. (1991) conducted a study on "The Spot Study of the Implementation of Vocationalisation of Education Programme in the State of Maharashtra". The study identified some inadequacies such as lack of suitable instructional materials, inadequacy of non-job training and non-recognition of vocational courses for employment.

Patel, S.P. (1991) studied "The Work Experience Programme in Secondary Teacher College". The study revealed that the facilities provided in terms of equipment, tools, workshop, trained teachers and funds were grossly inadequate. The time devoted to teaching its content and methodology too was inadequate.

Guru, G.Dhote A.K. and **Ray, S.** (1992) made a study on "The Spot Study of the Implementation of Vocationalisation of Education Programme in the State of Andhra Pradesh". It was found that although the programme received a boost with the introduction of the centrally sponsored scheme, it suffered from many deficiencies at the state level, viz. delay in creation of the management structure at different levels, lack of monitoring and inadequate linkage, infrastructure and on-the-job training. No modification in the recruitment rules non-recognition of vocational courses for employment and absence of follow-up of vocational graduates were other major reasons adversely affecting the programme. The study identified the presence of some committed teachers, innovative practices and dynamic Heads of the Institutions on the silver linings in the process of implementation.

Joshi, L.N. (1992) conducted a study on "Vocational Achievement and Problems Faced by the Students after passing the +2 Vocational Examinations". The study found that:

1. No Students could get loans from any agency;
2. A large number of students expressed that the theory portion of the vocational curriculum was very difficult;
3. Practical training was inadequate due to lack of tools, equipment and material;
4. Lack of desired competencies and insecurity of ta[illegible].

Swain, B.C. (1992) undertook a study on "Socially Useful Productive Work Experiences Programme at the Secondary Stage in Himachal Pradesh". The study identified certain weaknesses in programme implementation like teachers, non provision of in service training, non-availability of instructional material.

Sundara Rajan S.L. Sarah Santhan Kumari (1993) made a study on "Teachers Attitude towards Vocational Education in the Higher Secondary Schools in Tamil Nadu". The study found that by and large these teachers were favourably disposed towards it and except in a few cases, there was no significant difference between any two of their in respect of they attitude towards vocational education.

Bajaj, K.K. (1995) conducted a study on "Vocationalism - the challenge ahead". He found:

1. Inadequacy of resources, lack of trained man power to teach the courses, non-availability of reading material;
2. Many courses did not enjoy convenient and natural flowing linkages with the average academic level of +2 students who were to take these courses at +3 level.

Rashmi Agarwal and Indrakala (1996) made a study on "the Level of Vocational Aspirations of High School Students". It was found that:

1. Idealistic and realistic vocational aspiration levels of high school students were positively correlated but significantly different. These students had higher level ideals for therefore these future vocations the level of aspiration lowers door.
2. The concept that boys had higher level of vocational aspirations when compared to girls was not traced.
3. The level of vocational aspiration was not altered by their locality.

Sethumadhava Rao P.H. (1996) made a study on "Vocationalisation of First Degree Education". It was found that:

1. The context of the non-vocational subjects that a students would choose.

2. The employment potential has to be given top priority so that the students can get both theoretical and practical knowledge and will be successful in their ventures. The four important components of the scheme relating to vocational courses are:

   (a) Preparation of reading material for the teachers and students;

   (b) Training the teachers;

   (c) Monitoring and evaluation; and

   (d) Creating awareness of the programme among the Public through media etc.

Rajneesh Krishna and Bihay Kumar Pattnaik (1998) conducted a study on "the Impact of Education on Occupational Alignment: A Study in an Urban Community". It was found that: The parents from occupational category – 3 had a greater chance of sponsoring mobility of their wards as they largely could not influence the predictors of occupational mobility like medium of instruction, type of school and the place of school education. If they could ensure that their wards acquired professional education and could put in enough years of education, they would have a higher probability of attaining high prestige occupation. It can thus be concluded that among all the determinants of education, level of education has been found to be the most crucial in relation to occupational attainment.

Santosh Behera (1999) made a study on "Vocational Interests of +2 girls". It was found that:

1. Girls of science stream were found to have significantly better interest than the girls of humanities stream.

2. No significant difference was there between girls of science and humanities in literacy, persuasive, social device, artistic, teaching and home arrangement activities.

Raja Kumar Yadav (2000) conducted a study on "The vocational Preferences of Adolescents in Relation to their Intelligence and Achievement". It was found that:

1. The level of intelligence influences the vocational preference to a great extent.
2. High Achievement and low achievement science students differ significantly in their vocational preference in the same areas.
3. Achievement also influences the preference to a great extent.

Rameshwari Pandya (2000) made a study on "Vocationalisation of Education". He reported that:

1. The acceptability of Vocational courses would make students get suitable employment after completion of the training hence rules of recruitment in Government, Public and Private Sectors need to be amended.
2. In vocational training the cost per student was very high when compared to general education.
3. An attempt should be made for an alternative strategy for vocational education, which is not exclusively school based on formal in nature.

Qureshi, M.N. (2001) made a study on "National Vocational Qualifications (NVO's) — An Approach towards Meeting the Global Skill Needs". He stated that National Vocational Qualifications (NVO's) would open new access in the all round development of a person. The technical institutions like, industrial training institutes and polytechnics have a great scope to play an important role in the NVO's system.

Sehgal, G.S. (2001) in his book Work Education suggested that the improvement of work experience programme in schools include:

1. Principals of active participation in the implementation of work experience programme;

2. Proper allotment of work experience activities according to the aptitude of students;
3. More training programmes for teachers;
4. Availability of raw material to schools; and
5. Proper motivation of teachers and students.

Prasantha Kumar, M.V. (2002) made a study on "Vocationalisation an Overview" and found that the purpose of on-the-job training was to make students familiar with the atmosphere and problem of actual working conditions. Study tour, coaching, apprenticeship, job rotation, special assignments etc. were the important methods of successful vocational training on-the-job training aids and techniques, such as charts, lecture, manuals, oral and written explanations, demonstrations, audio and video tapes and other aids. Therefore, specialization in every branch of study was essential for a better placement. Here he stressed the relevance of job-oriented vocational education, which would equip also a young man for self-employment leading to a betterment of their standard of living.

REVIEWS RELATED TO VOCATIONAL EDUCATION (SPECIAL EDUCATION)

Paul, D. Geyer and **John, G. Schroeder** (1919) studied the "Conditions Influencing the Availability of Accommodations for Workers Who were Deaf or Hard of Hearing". They noticed that an accommodation was more likely to be available for participants with higher levels of education and for those in professional or managerial occupations.

Misra, S.K. and **Misra, S.D.** (1967) conducted a study on "Vocational Rehabilitation through Guidance Services for a Deaf, Physically Handicapped." They found that:

1. The vocational counseling would help the deaf individual to ascertain, accept, understand and apply the relevant facts about himself and about the occupational world which were ascertained through incidental and planned activation.

2. The vocational counseling services would also help the individual to develop the rehabilitation vocational corner.

Muthiah, P.N. (1989) made a study on "Vocational Education for the Disable in Tamil Nadu - A Survey". He found that the vocational training imparted was not in accordance with the interests and aspirations of the children.

Uma Devi, L. and **Venkata Ramaiah, P.** (1991) made a study on "A Study on Attitudes and Aspirations of Parents Towards their Deaf Children". It was found that:

1. Sixty per cent of the parents expressed high expectations from their deaf children by expecting good job in future.
2. Eighty-three per cent of parents expressed but they had received help from the welfare agencies for rehabilitation, for job placement and better resource facilities and for finance.

Krishna Chandra and **Aran Banik** (1992) made a study on "A Study of Indigenous Vocational Evaluation System for the Hearing Impaired Persons". The findings of the study include:

1. The hearing impaired who performed in a better way and showed the quality of work, had basic educational background and knowledge.
2. Vocational training and CDP in relation to the educational performance were significant at 0.001.

Chandramani, M. and **Kalaivani, M.** (1993) in their study "Survey of Educational Facilities Available for Deaf Children" found that there was scarcity of vocational teachers in many vocational courses like tailoring, painting and type writing which were taught in many schools.

Marjatt Takala (1994) conducted a study on "Deaf Finish Adults' views of their Society, Knowledge, Satisfaction, Values and Attitudes". It was found that the deaf adults expressed higher level of satisfaction with government services for the deaf and wages provided for them by the government.

David A, Steward, John F, Vinsonhaler and **Leighton Price** (1995) in their study on "the Decisions by Teachers and Computer on Deaf and Hard of Hearing Placement" pointed out that the three generic features were aggregated together by a teacher of deaf students to make placement decisions.

Denna J Sands, Lois Adms and **Donna M, Stout** (1995) in their study on "A Statewide Exploration of the Nature and Use of Curriculum in Special Education" found that, the teachers wanted training in teaching compensatory skills and life skills, and teacher focus on academic remediation versus life-skill, self advocacy, vocational or strategy instruction.

Laird W, Heal and **Frank R, Rush** (1995) made a study on "Predicting Employment for Students who have Special Education in High School Programs", and concluded that employment, student competence and family characteristics had been controlled statistically.

Sharon Hall Defur and **Juliana M, Taymans** (1995) made a study on "Competencies Needed for Transition Specialists in Vocational Rehabilitation, Vocational Education, and Special Education" found that the knowledge of agencies and system change had the highest rate of competency.

Suson Brown Zahn and **Laura, J. Kely** (1995) made a study on "Changing Attitudes about the Employability of the Deaf and Hard of Hearing". The study revealed that deaf and hard of hearing individuals who were employed in a variety of occupational settings played a significant role and showed positive attitude about their employability.

Dayl L, Scherich (1996) in his study of "Job Accommodations in the Work Place for Persons who are Deaf or Hard of Hearing, Current Practices and Recommendations" observed that both employers and workers had lack of knowledge about appropriate accommodation options and benefits derived from those accommodations.

Denetta, L. Dowler and **Richard, T. Walls** (1996) made a study on "Accommodating Specific Job Functions for People with Hearing Impairments". It was found that people with Hearing Impairment were under employed and over respected in unskilled labour jobs.

Jean Whitney-Thomas and **Cheryl Hanley-Maxwell** (1996) studied on "Packing the Parachute: Parent's Experiences on their children Prepared to leave High School" and pointed out that the parents of students with disabilities showed greater discomfort and had less optimistic vision about their disabled Sons and Daughter's future than the parents of students without disabilities.

James, R. Patton, May E. Cronin and **Veda Jajprrels** (1997) studied on "Curricular Implication of Transition life Skills Instruction on a Integral part of Transition Education". They pointed that the educational programs of many students in Special Education were not meeting their current or future needs.

Laird, W. Heal, Madhob Khoju and **Frank, R. Rush** (1997) conducted a study on "Predicting Quality of Life of Youths after they leave Special Education High School Programs". They found that many able competent young individuals tend to disappear from disability service networks soon after high school education.

Paul, D. Geyer and **John, G. Schroeder** (1999) both made a study on "Early Career Job Satisfaction for Full time Workers who are Deaf or Hard of Hearing", and found that workers who were Deaf and Hard of Hearing made decisions to seek another job based on their level of job satisfaction.

Mery. C. Holter and **Maria. C. Dinis** (2001) studied on "Self-esteem Enhancement in Deaf and Hearing Women, Success Stories". They said that education and employment were the two factors which helped in the enhancement of their self-esteem.

Kathy Whenler-Scruggs (2002) in his study on "Assessing the Employment and Independence of People Who are Deaf and Low Functioning" found that the service providers who were assisting the people of deaf and low functioning needed to educate and train them regarding the issues of work behaviours, ethics, benefits and independent living skills.

Favidah Serjul Haq (2003) made a study on "Career and Employment Opportunities for Women with Disabilities in Malaysia" and concluded that employment for Women with disability was important for the following reasons:

1. for economic independence and successful living;
2. for a sense of self worth, dignity and contribution to Society; and
3. for integration into the mainstream of non-disabled community.

Govinda Rao, L. and **Siva Kumar, T.C.** (2003) in their research article "Vocational Training of the Mentally Retorted" stated that, it was vital to standardize the vocational training on a course with standard curricle for various traders. It is essential to see that the persons with mental retardation are placed in open employment situations, and to see that the persons with mental retardation live a qualitative life independently and in the community known and should level with them.

Madan Kundu Alo Datta, Chrisarm Schira - Geist and **Lee Crandall** (2003) made a study on "Disability Related Services: Needs and Satisfaction of Postsecondary Students". Higher need for high quality support services to improve the accessibility of institutions of higher education for students with disabilities was felt.

Anand, S.P. (2003) in his article "Guidance and Counselling for Vocational Education in Schools" said that the need for vocational education both generic and specific – had been accepted by all stakeholders of education. The spread of vocational education and its effective implementation could be achieved by guidance and counselling.

Veena Easvara Doss, Sumathi, D. and **Rekha, B.** (2005) conducted a study on "Career Decision - Making Self-efficacy among High School Adolescents". It was found that the girls of 11th standard showed higher levels of self-efficiency in career decision making.

SUMMARY

- The vocational courses which are at present run are useful when compared to the general courses. But they have failed to prepare the students for job or self-employment.
- The government has not provided sufficient financial assistance to the students passing out with vocational courses.
- The problems encountered by the schools in implementing the socially useful productive work include non availability of specialised teachers, inadequate physical and infrastructure facilities, non-supply of syllabus copies, lack of guidelines for the disposal of finished products.
- Very few schools are imparting vocational education
- No Placement service wing.
- Teachers who are teaching vocational courses are untrained and inadequate.
- Rural students showed interest in science built courses, but are not interested in agriculture built courses.
- Art and commerce students expressed much interest in executive and in white-colour jobs. They are against physical labour.
- The in service teacher training programmes organised are grossly inadequate.
- No Provision is made for raw materials and other contingencies.
- Boys are being introduced to vocational courses at the secondary stage rather than senior secondary stage.
- Inadequacies and drawbacks in the implementation of the centrally sponsored scheme of vocationalisation of (CSS) secondary education include inadequacy of institutions,

management structure, and selection of courses, curriculum design, and instruction materials.

- No vocational guidance is provided to students.
- Inadequacy of equipment, tools, workshops, trained teacher funds and shortage of time to teach content and methodology.
- Lack of monitoring and inadequate linkage, and infrastructure, non-recognition of vocational courses for employment.
- The cost of vocational training is very high when compared to general education.
- Proper allotment of work experience activities according to aptitude of students.
- Scarcity of vocational teachers in many schools.
- Teachers want training in teaching compensatory skills and life skills.
- Teacher focused on academic remediation versus life-skill, self advocacy and Vocational instruction.
- Lack of knowledge about appropriate accommodation options and benefits.
- H.I one under employed and over expected in unskilled labour jobs.
- Educational programmes of many students in special education are not meeting their current or future needs.
- Many differently able young individuals tend to disappear from disability service network soon after high school education.
- Accommodations are more likely to be available for participants with higher levels of education and for those in professional or managerial occupations.

- Vocational training imparted to the disabled is not in accordance with the interests and aspirations of the children.
- Parents expressed the need for help from welfare agencies for rehabilitation, Job placement and better resource facilities and finance.
- Deaf and hard of hearing individuals who are employed in a variety of occupational settings play a significant role and showed positive attitude about their employability.
- Education and employment will help in the enhancement of deaf and hearing women self-esteem.
- Deaf and low functioning individuals need to be educated and trained with issues regarding work behaviours, ethics benefits and independent living skills.
- Career and employment opportunity for women with disabilities is important for economic independence, self worth dignity for integration into the mainstream of non-disabled community.

APPRAISAL

The conclusions drawn from the review of literature, it is obvious that studies were done in that career of employment opportunities, life skills, socially useful productive work and vacationed rehabilitation etc., were considered but not vocational education at secondary school level for the Hearing Impaired. This lacuna has created a necessity to select the topic for the study. The variables objectives were selected in such a way that they would strengthen part of the Review of the Literature.

SECTION - II

CHAPTER 4

PRESENT STUDY ON VOCATIONAL EDUCATION IMPARTED TO THE HEARING IMPAIRED STUDENTS

Review of related literature oriented the Researcher towards the possible areas of research in the field. The author framed the objectives, Research questions, Hypotheses from the conclusions drawn. The methodology of the study was planned accordingly. This chapter contains the methodology of the study.

There are different methods of research that are very commonly used in the field of education. The difference in the methodology is largely due to the difference in purpose and approach only.

Keeping in view the scope and purpose of the study, the present investigator has preferred normative survey method as a method of research in this investigation.

This chapter describes procedure followed in the collection of the data, the construction of the tool, pilot studies, administration of the tool and statistical techniques used for analysis.

STATEMENT OF THE PROBLEM

The presents study is entitled as **"Vocational Education of Hearing Impaired Students"**.

OBJECTIVES OF THE STUDY

The following objectives are set for the purpose of the study:

1. To identity the vocational needs of hearing impaired students at secondary school level in Andhra Pradesh from the point of view of:
   (a) Teachers; and
   (b) Students.
2. To identify the Vocational Courses offered by the special schools to the hearing impaired children at secondary school level in Andhra Pradesh.
3. To Study the existing facilities in special schools for hearing impaired students at secondary level with reference to:
   (a) Infrastructure; and
   (b) Financial Support.
4. To study the ways and means of imparting vocational education to hearing impaired students in special schools at secondary level, with reference to:
   (a) Course Content;
   (b) Strategies of Teaching;
   (c) Duration;
   (d) Evaluation;
   (e) Certification; and
   (f) Vocational Trained Teachers.
5. To study about the Job opportunities for the qualified hearing impaired students who received vocational education.

RESEARCH QUESTIONS

For conducting the smooth research, the following research questions were set up

1. Do the special children need vocational education?
2. What are the different vocational education courses introduced to hearing impaired students in special schools at secondary level in AP?
3. What are the facilities available to impart vocational education to hearing impaired students in secondary school in AP?
4. How is vocational Education imparted to the Hearing impaired students in special schools at secondary level?
5. What are the Job opportunities available to the hearing impaired students.

The above Research questions posed in the investigation served as major investigation areas, out of which specific hypotheses were formulated for further investigation to find out the status of vocational courses in the schools meant for the deaf, at secondary level.

HYPOTHESES FOR THE STUDY

Based on the above objectives, the following hypotheses were set for the study:

1. There is no significant difference in the expressed responses of the teachers on the "Usefulness of Vocational Education Courses Offered in the schools to take up Jobs in Future" with respect to Region, Gender and type of management.
2. There is no significant difference in the responses of the teachers as the "Receipt of Financial Assistance is Adequate to Conduct Vocational Education Courses" with respect to Region, Gender and Management.
3. There is no significant difference in the expressed responses of the teachers on the "Different Working Hours for

Vocational Courses are Sufficient" with reference to Region, Gender and Type of Management.

4. There is no significant difference in the expressed responses of the teachers on "Minimum pass marks in Vocational Education Courses" with respect to Region, Gender and Type of Management.
5. There is no significant difference in the expressed responses of the teacher on "Courage of all Aspects Pertaining to Vocational Education in the Curriculum" with reference to Region, Gender and Type of Management
6. There is no significant difference in the expressed responses of the teachers on the "Carefulness of Vocational Education Certificates in getting jobs" with respect to Region, Gender, and Management of the school.
7. There is no significant difference in the expressed responses of the teachers on the "Usefulness of Training Programmes in Vocational Education Courses" with respect to Region, Gender and Type of Management.
8. There is no significant difference in the expressed responses of the Hearing Impaired students on the "Availability of Sufficient room for Vocational Education Courses" with reference to Region, Gender and Management of the school.
9. There is no significant difference in the expressed responses of the students on the "Availability of Adequate Machinery for Vocational Education Courses" with reference to Region, Gender and Type of Management.
10. There is no significant difference in the expressed responses of the students on "Availability of Adequate Number of Computers", with reference to Region, Gender and Type of Management.
11. There is no significant difference in the expressed responses of the students, on "Taking up Self-employment after

Completion of Vocational Education Courses" with reference to Region, Gender and Management of the school.

12. There is no significant difference in the expressed responses of the students, on the "Economic Utility of the Vocational Courses" with respect to Region, Gender and Management of the school.

DESIGN

To study the present problem the investigator selected the normative survey method, which concerns itself with the present phenomena in terms of conditions, practice, belief, process, relationships or trends that are going on, termed as "Normative survey or descriptive survey or survey". Existing worthwhile survey studies collect three types of information:

1. Of what exists?
2. Of what we want?
3. Of how to get these?

In the present study the investigator adopted the normative survey method to study, and describe the existing vocational education in special schools for the deaf in Andhra Pradesh and interpret the existing vocational education phenomenon, and its status. The investigator also made an attempt and provided an understanding about the significance of vocational education especially to the hearing impaired.

SAMPLE

It is a process by which a relatively small number of individuals or measures of individuals, objects or events are selected or analysed in order to find-out something about the entire population of the universe from which it was selected.

In the present study the purposive random sampling technique was employed.

Schools

In the present study, 20 special schools for the Deaf were identified from the three regions of Andhra Pradesh namely Coastal Andhra, Telangana, and Rayalaseema, out of which 8 were State Government schools and 12 schools were of Private Management including aided and unaided.

The schools were selected keeping in view the regional criteria, and the level. The regional criterion was kept in view because the preference for the vocations may be influenced by the regions, the number of schools depended on the availability of the high schools. The high schools for the hearing impaired were minimum. So all the high schools for the hearing impaired identified were taken for the study. The addresses of the schools were collected from audiologists, and speech therapists, special education departments of various universities, disabled welfare department, and schools for the Hearing impaired.

Students

For the purpose of studying the vocational education imparted to hearing impaired students in Andhra Pradesh, from the selected 20 schools a representative sample of 600 hearing impaired students were selected through purposive random sampling procedure from the three regions of Andhra Pradesh, namely, Coastal Andhra, Telangana, and Rayalaseema equally distributed among VIII, IX and X class covering both the sexes. The students of secondary school were selected for the study based on the following reasons i.e.

1. Students of secondary school could comprehend the questions, and they were able to react to them quickly when compared to primary school students.
2. Communication becomes easier after primary school age.
3. This mental maturity level was high and they could select the future courses formerly and easily.
4. Students who were regular to the school based on their attendance 10 students were chosen from the each class i.e. 8th, 9th and 10th for the study.

5. Lastly, the vocationalization of school education is limited only to secondary and senior secondary level in AP.

Teachers

A sample of 145 teachers who were working in special schools and 600 students were included for the purpose of study. The teachers and students from three regions of Andhra Pradesh were included who comprised specially trained and vocational trained and general trained teachers working in special secondary schools for the deaf. (Table 4.1 and fig. 4.1)

Table 4.1: Distribution of Samples

S. No.	*Variable*	*Groups*	*Teachers*	*Total*	*Students*	*Total*
1.	Region	Coastal Andhra	58		240	
		Telangana	67		270	
		Rayalaseema	20	**145**	90	**600**
2.	Gender	Male	66		395	
		Female	79	**145**	215	**600**
3.	Management	Government	67		240	
		Private	78	**145**	360	**600**

TOOLS

1. Questionnaire

The present study is aimed at to collect the data for the study the investigator used questionnaire and a schedule. The investigator used two types of questionnaires - one for students and another for teachers.

Schedule

A schedule was also prepared according to experts' suggestions and used by the investigator, to collect the required data.

ANDHRA PRADESH

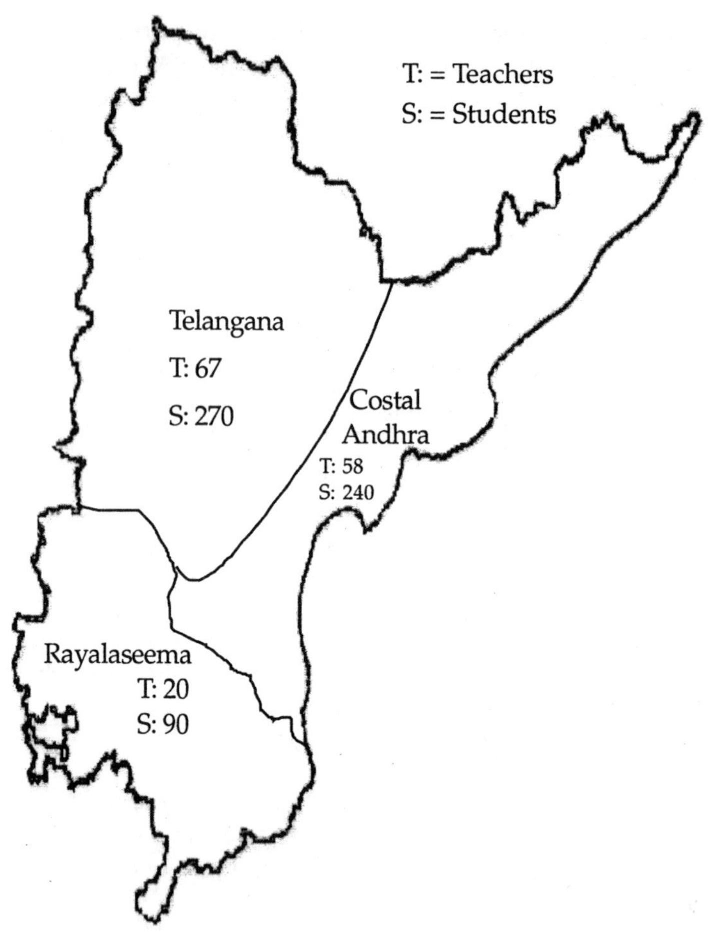

Fig. 4.1: **Diagramatically Distribution of Samples of Andhra Pradesh**

CONSTRUCTION OF THE PRELIMINARY FORM OF THE QUESTIONNAIRE

A preliminary form of the questionnaire was constructed by taking the opinion of the students studying in schools for deaf, teachers working in special schools for deaf and special Educators. The researcher herself identified some of the aspects through personal observation and experience and framed some questions. The framed questions were supplemented by a careful study of related literature and discussion with experts in the field of special education. The collected information was refined by observing the following criteria:

- Clarity, precision and straight forwardness of the words used in the questions.
- Short and pin-pointed expressions.
- Avoiding double barrel questions.
- Avoiding/Evading double negatives in a question.

The pool of questions thus refined were presented to the experienced in the field of research and especially in the field of special education with reference to hearing impaired and requested to:

- Add other questions relevant to the subject.
- Point out redundant questions.
- Mark ambiguous and double-barrelled questions.

In view of their suggestions some more questions were included in the questionnaire and some questions were deleted. Accordingly the final refined tool was prepared.

PILOT STUDY

The Telugu Version of the Questionnaire was administered on a representative sample of 150 of Hearing Impaired students and 50 teachers selected with stratified random sample of 3 special schools for the Deaf in three regions, which represents the three geographical regions viz., Coastal Andhra (Vijayawada) Telangana (Miryalaguda) and Rayalaseema (Tirupati) of Andhra Pradesh.

While administrating the questionnaire, the selected subjects were instructed and motivated in answering the questions. The purpose of the test was explained and sufficient time was give to them and they were assured that their responses would be kept under confidential and would be used only for research purpose.

RELIABILITY OF THE QUESTIONNAIRE

Reliability of a test is the consistency with which a test measures a trait for which it is intended. According to Garret (Garrett, 1971), "A test score is called reliable when we have reason for believing the score to be stable and trustworthy".

The reliability of any tool can be established by different methods like test-retest method, split-half method and alternate forms method. In the present study the investigator adopted test-retest method to establish the reliability of the tools.

To study the independent nature of the test items, the hearing impaired students of 8th, 9th and 10th classes and teachers working in special school for the deaf were selected and separate questionnaire was administered to them. After 30 days, again the investigator gave the questionnaire to the same group of students as well as the teachers and answers were compared with the previous responses for consistency. The correlation co-efficient between the two sets of scores is 0.63 which is significant at 0.01 level. Hence the questionnaire may be considered as having high degree of reliability.

VALIDITY

The second important characteristic of a good tool is its validity. This form of validity is estimated by evaluating the relevance of the test items individually and as a whole. Each of the items/statements should be relevant on the psychological concept being measured, and all the items statements put together should cover the entire range of the concept.

According to Thorndike, R.N. and Elizabeth Hagen (1970) "Validity refers to the extent to which a test measures what we actually wish to measure."

To determine the validity of the developed tool the content validity has been established.

Content Validity

The content validity refers to the degree to which a test sample of the content area is to be measured. Content validity is essentially based upon the judgement of the expert. In the present questionnaires a systematic effort was made by the investigator to examine the test items related to the objectives of the study. While preparing the tools the investigator consulted the experts in the field of education and special education. There was much consensus among the experts regarding the selection of items. Most of them were accepted as they were, a few items were modified according to their suggestions. Thus it can be reasonably assumed that the administered tools have content validity.

Item Validity

Item validity stresses the number of discriminations of the desired sort that the item is capable of making. It stresses the extent to which the item of the present such has been established as explained earlier. Thus the items chosen for the questionnaire have been found to be satisfactorily valid.

Intrinsic Validity

According to Guilford (1954) intrinsic validity indicates the degree to which the test measures what it purports to measure. It is also defined as the mount of true variance in the obtained scores or how well the obtained scores measures the test true scores component. Intrinsic validity of a test is expressed items of square root of its reliability value. Hence the intrinsic validity of the tool is as follows. The questionnaires reliability co-efficient is 0.63.Therefore the intrinsic validity is:

$\sqrt{0.63} = 0.79.$

Thus the validity of the tool is justified.

FINALISATION OF THE TOOL

For finalising the questionnaire after establishing reliability and validity the views of some experienced teachers who were working in the schools for the Deaf, Special Educators and suggestions of the research guide were taken into consideration. The final form of the questionnaire is appended under appendices.

DATA COLLECTION

The investigator personally visited each institution selected for the sample and obtained permission from the respective heads of the institutions. The subjects identified, for the study were briefed about the purpose of the study and the need for their involvement infusing valid information in conducting the study in a scientific way.

Before administering the questionnaire, the hearing impaired students as well as teachers were informed about the nature and importance of the investigation. They were requested to be sincere in their response and to cooperate in the successful completion of the work. The investigator specially emphasized that the responses supplied by them would be kept strictly confidential. The questionnaires were distributed in their classes and the instructions were given to the students which they read silently for themselves. Doubts were clarified and they were asked to mark their responses by placing tick (✓) mark against their choice from the respective alternatives given against each item and to give their response for open ended questions they were given ample time.

A separate questionnaire was administered to the teachers in the special school for the Deaf. Before administering the tool the teachers were also informed about the nature, purpose and significance of the study, and specially emphasized that the responses supplied by them would be kept strictly confidential. They were asked to respond to all the items by placing a tick (✓) mark against their choice from the respective alternatives given against each item and give their response to open ended questions.

The tool was self responding however; the procedure for filling the tool was explained. Doubts raised by the teachers were clarified and they were asked to mark their responses to different items. Further the respondents were requested not to leave any item in the questionnaire unanswered. They were also requested to return the filled-in forms on the same day. The investigator as per the given time met the teachers personally and obtained the filled in forms.

ANALYSIS OF THE DATA

The data collected was analysed using relevant statistical techniques such as frequencies, percentages and chi-squares.

- The frequencies of responses to the various items in the questionnaire were tabulated.
- The frequencies were converted into percentages.
- Chi-square was calculated.

The obtained results were graphically presented by diagrammatic representation wherever necessary.

CHAPTER 5

ANALYSIS AND INTERPRETATION ON VOCATIONAL EDUCATION IMPARTED TO THE HEARING IMPAIRED STUDENTS

In the present chapter the data collected were systematically classified and tabulated as per the formulated Research Questions, and hypothesis. The data were analysed and interpreted to draw the conclusions from the study. The outcome of the analyses was interpreted in the light of the limitations of the data collected. The analysis and interpretation of the data involves the objectives of the study to be derived from the collected data including the internal meaning and their relation to the problem.

According to Ferguson, G.A. (1981):

"the process of interpretation is essentially one of the stating: what the result show, what do they mean, what is their significance, what is the answer to the original problem."

It is essential while interpreting the results secured after a statistical analysis of complex data, to test whether the observed values or difference in statistics are all significant, and are not caused by chance errors of sampling or not. If significant, how significant they are?

ANALYSIS OF THE DATA

The data collected from the teachers who were working in school for the deaf and the Hearing impaired from the students studying in schools for the deaf in the regions of Andhra Pradesh were analysed.

Imparting Vocational Education Along with General Education

To know the responses of the teacher towards imparting vocational education along with general education, the investigator collected the data and analysed with the help the percentage and the results presented in Table 5.1.

Table 5.1: Imparting Vocational Education along with General Education

Sl. No.	*Importing Vocational Education*	*Region*			*Gender*		*Management*	
		Coastal Andhra	*Telan-gana*	*Rayala-seema*	*Male*	*Female*	*Govt.*	*Private*
1.	Yes	36.2% (21)	46.2% (31)	75% (15)	45.4% (30)	46.8% (37)	38.8% (26)	51.3% (40)
2.	No	63.8% (37)	53.7% (36)	25% (5)	54.5% (36)	53.1% (42)	61.1% (41)	48.7% (38)
	Total	**58**	**67**	**20**	**66**	**79**	**67**	**78**

Table 5.2 shows that from all the three regions of Andhra Pradesh the majority of the Teachers (75%) of Rayalaseema expressed that they were imparting vocational education courses along with general education whereas in contrast more number of Coastal Andhra (CA) and Telangana (T) teachers (A - 63.8%,

T - 53.7%) responded that they were not providing vocational education along with the general education at recorded level in special schools.

With reference to gender variable both men and women (Male (M)- 54.5%, Female (F) - 53.1%) equally expressed that the special schools were not providing vocational education along with the general education whereas 45.4% of men and 46.8% of women responded that they were providing vocational education along with the general education.

When we consider the management variable, the majority of the teachers from Government schools (61.1%) expressed that they were not imparting vocational educational along with the general education. In contrast the teachers from private schools (51.3%) expressed that they were providing vocational education along with the general education.

This finding supports the view of Mohanty G. (1986) "A Survey on Vocational Education of Orissa" which correlates with the finding that very few schools are imparting Vocational Education.

Different Types of Vocational Education Courses Provided by the Schools

To know what type of vocational courses imparted to the schools, the investigator analysed the collected data with the help the percentage of their responses on the questionnaire and the results obtained are presented in Table 5.2.

From Table 5.2 it is obvious that more number of teachers from Coastal Andhra, Telangana and Rayalaseema responded that they were offering Tailoring (CA - 82.7%, T - 53.7%, R - 65%), Book binding (A - 65.5%, T - 46.3%, R - 65%), Computer courses (A - 20.7%, T - 46.3%, R - 65%), Candle/Basket making (CA - 13.8%, T - 7.5%, R - 3.4%) and Typewriting (CA - 10.3%, T - 9%, R - 25%), whereas a least number of teachers from Coastal Andhra, Telangana expressed that they were offering TV/Radio mechanism (CA - 10.3%, T - 2.9%) and Carpentry (CA - 25.9%, T - 1.5%). Only teachers from Andhra responded that they offered Domestic wiring (12%).

Table 5.2: Different Types of Vocational Education Courses provided by the Schools

S. No.	*Vocational Educational Courses*	*Region*			*Gender*		*Management*	
		Coastal Andhra	*Telangana*	*Rayalaseema*	*Male*	*Female*	*Govt.*	*Private*
1.	Tailoring	82.7% (48)	53.7% (36)	65% (13)	77.3% (51)	57% (45)	62.6% (42)	67.9% (53)
2.	Book-binding	65.5% (38)	46.3% (31)	65% (13)	59.7% (40)	53.1% (42)	56.7% (38)	56.4% (44)
3.	Typewriting	10.3% (6)	9% (6)	25% (5)	12.1% (8)	11.3% (9)	10.4% (7)	12.8% (10)
4.	Carpentry	25.9% (15)	1.5% (1)	-	16.6% (11)	6.3% (5)	14.9% (10)	7.6% (6)
5.	Computer (Hardware/ Software)	20.7% (12)	11.9% (8)	35% (7)	22.7% (15)	15.1% (12)	7.4% (5)	28.2% (22)
6.	TV/Radio Mechanism	10.3% (6)	2.9% (2)	-	7.6% (5)	3.8% (3)	-	10.2% (8)
7.	Domestic wiring	12% (7)	-	-	6% (4)	3.7% (3)	-	8.9% (7)
8.	Candle Basket making	13.8% (8)	7.5% (5)	3.4% (5)	15.1% (10)	10.1% (8)	14.9% (10)	10.2% (8)

Note: The teacher's responses are for more than one vocational training.

With reference to gender variable, both men and women teachers offered Vocational Education courses like Tailoring (M - 77.3%, F-57%), Book-binding (M - 59.7%, F - 53.1%), Computer (M - 22.7%, F - 15.1%), Typewriting (M - 12.1%, F - 11.3%), Carpentry (M - 16.6%, F - 6.3%), Candle/Basket making (M - 15.1%, F - 10.1%), T.V./Radio Mechanism (M - 7.6%, F - 3.8%) and Domestic wiring (M - 6%, W - 3.7%).

The management variable reveals that teachers working in both government and private management schools offered vocational education courses like tailoring (G - 62.6%, P - 67.9%), Book binding (G - 56.7%, P - 56.4%) candle/Basket making (G - 14.2%, P - 10.2%), Computers (G - 7.4%, P - 28.2%), Carpentry (G - 14.9%, P - 7.6%) and Typewriting (G - 10.4%, P - 12.8%), whereas only private schools are offering TV/Radio mechanism (10.2%) and Domestic wiring (8.9%) than the other schools.

Regionwise Responses of the Teachers on the Usefulness of Vocational Education Courses Offered in Taking up Jobs

To know regionwise responses of the teachers on the "usefulness of vocational education courses offered in taking up jobs, the investigator analysed the collected data with the help the chi-square test and the results obtained are presented in Table 5.3.

Table 5.3: The Regionwise Responses of the Teachers on the "Usefulness of Vocational Education Courses Offered in Taking up Jobs"

Regions in A.P.	*Yes*	*No*	*Total*	χ^2
Coastal Andhra	14	44	58	0.952**
Telangana	17	50	67	
Rayalaseema	7	13	20	
Total	**38**	**107**	**145**	

** Not significant.

Hypothesis

There is no significant region wise difference in the responses of the teachers with respect to the "Usefulness of Vocational Education courses offered in the schools in taking up jobs in future".

The data in Table 5.3 show that the calculated chi-square value of the responses of the region wise teachers is 0.952 which is less than the table value of 5.99 and not is significant at 0.05 level. Therefore, it can be stated that the region of the teachers do not have any significant value on their responses with regard to the usefulness of the Vocational Education in taking up their jobs. Hence it can be said that the formulated hypothesis is accepted.

It is evident that the majority of the teachers from all the three regions (107 out of 145) stated that the vocational courses being offered presently in their schools were not useful to take up jobs in future. Only some teachers (38 out of 145) have opined that the vocational courses were useful.

This needs a special consideration on the part of the government to visualise the right aspect of vocational courses.

The Responses of the Teachers Genderwise on the Usefulness of Vocational Education Courses in Taking up Jobs

To know the responses of the teachers gender wise on the "Usefulness of Vocational Education courses in taking up jobs, the investigator analysed the collected data with the help of chi-square test and the results obtained are presented in Table 5.4.

Hypothesis

There is no significant difference in the gender wise responses of the teachers with respect to the "Usefulness of vocational education courses offered in their schools in taking up jobs in future to the hearing impaired students".

Table 5.4: The responses of the Teachers genderwise on the Usefulness of Vocational Education Courses in taking up Jobs

Gender	*Yes*	*No*	*Total*	χ^2
Male	15	51	66	
Female	23	56	79	0.464**
Total	**38**	**107**	**145**	

** Not significant.

From Table 5.4 it is noticed that the calculated Chi-square (χ^2) value of the gender wise responses of the teachers is 0.464 which is less than the table value of 3.841 and not significant at 0.05 level. Therefore, it can be said that gender response of the teachers does not have any significant value with respect to the usefulness of the vocational education in taking up jobs. Hence, it can be stated that the formulated hypothesis is accepted.

Further the data reveal that both the male and female teachers (107 out of 145) responded that the vocational courses offered in their schools were not useful to take up jobs in future. Only some teachers 38 out of 145 teachers said that the vocational courses were useful to take up jobs in future.

This finding supports the view of Gokhale (1984) that the present vocational education courses failed to prepare the students for any job or self-employment.

The Responses of the Teachers in Relation to Management of the School on the Usefulness of Vocational Education Courses in Taking up Jobs

To know the responses of the teachers in relation to management of the school on the "Usefulness of vocational education courses in taking up jobs", the investigator analysed the collected data with the help of chi-square test and the results obtained are presented in Table 5.5.

Table 5.5: The responses of the teachers in relation to management of the school on the Usefulness of vocational education courses in taking up jobs

Management	*Yes*	*No*	*Total*	χ^2
Government	12	55	67	
Private	26	52	78	3.67*
Total	**38**	**107**	**145**	

* Significant.

Hypothesis

There is no significant difference in the responses of the teachers in relation to the management of the schools in which they are working, on the "Usefulness of vocational education courses offered in their schools in taking up jobs to the Hearing impaired students".

The calculated Chi-square value of the responses of the teachers in relation to management of the school i.e. both government and private in which they are working is 3.67 which is less than the table value of 3.841 at 0.05 level. Therefore it can be said that the teacher's responses from different management of schools do not have any significant value with regard to the usefulness of vocational education courses offered in their schools to take up jobs in future. Hence the hypothesis is retained.

The majority of the teachers (107 and of 145) working in both government and private management schools stated that the present vocational courses were not useful to take up jobs in future.

The Responses of the Teachers in Relation to Regionswise, Managementwise, Genderwise on the Usefulness of Vocational Education Courses in Taking up Jobs

To know the responses of the teachers in relation to regions wise, management wise, gender wise on the usefulness of vocational education courses in taking up jobs, the investigator analysed the collected data with the help the percentage of their responses on the questionnaire and the results obtained are presented in Table 5.6 and fig. 5.1.

Table 5.6: Suitable Vocations

Sl. No.	*Vocational Courses*	*Regions*			*Gender*		*Management*	
		Coastal Andhra	*Telan-gana*	*Rayala-seema*	*Male*	*Female*	*Govt.*	*Private*
1.	Tailoring	20.7% (12)	14.9% (10)	10% (2)	15.2% (10)	17.7% (14)	11.9% (8)	20.5% (16)
2.	Book-binding	12% (7)	18% (12)	20% (4)	12.1% (8)	19% (15)	13.4% (9)	17.9% (14)
3.	Type-writing	8.6% (5)	10.4% (7)	15% (3)	10.6% (7)	10% (8)	13.4% (9)	7.7% (6)
4.	TV/ Radio mechanism	8.6% (5)	9% (6)	10% (2)	9% (6)	8.9% (7)	11.9% (8)	6.4% (5)
5.	Computer (Hardware/Software)	25.9% (15)	27% (18)	30% (6)	19.7% (13)	32.9% (26)	23.9% (16)	29.4% (23)
6.	Carpentry training	13.7% (8)	18% (12)	10% (2)	22.7% (15)	8.9% (7)	17.9% (12)	12.8% (10)
7.	Domestic-wiring	10.3% (6)	3% (2)	5% (1)	10.6% (7)	2.5% (2)	7.5% (5)	5.1% (4)
	Total	**58**	**67**	**20**	**66**	**79**	**67**	**78**

Table 5.6 shows suitable vocational courses for the Hearing impaired. Most of the teachers from all the three regions favoured Computer courses (A-25.9%, T-27%, R-30%), Tailoring (A-20.7%, T-14.9%, R-10%), Book-binding (A-12%, T-18%, R-20%), Carpentry (A-13.8%, T-18%, R-10%). The rest of the teachers favoured Typewriting (A-8.6%, T-10.4%, R-15%), TV/Radio mechanism (A-8.6%, T-9%, R-10%) and Domestic wiring (A-10.3%, T-3%, R-5%).

With reference to Gender variable the majority of the male teachers favoured Carpentry (22.7%), Computer course (19.7%), Tailoring (15.2%), Book binding (12.1%), whereas the female

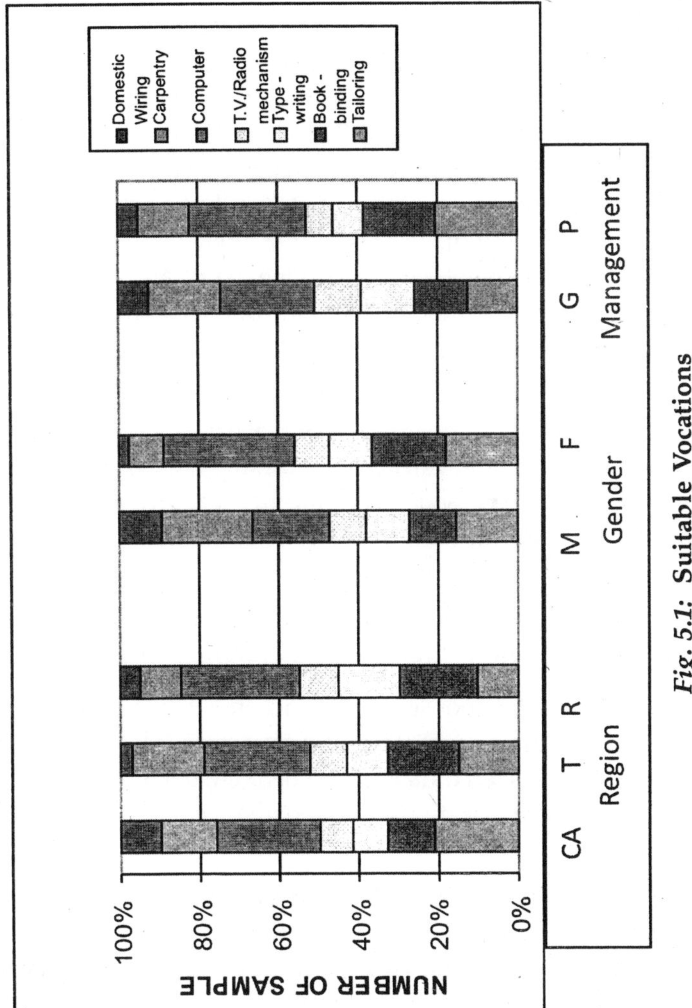

Fig. 5.1: **Suitable Vocations**

teachers preferred Computers (32.9%), Bookbinding (19%), Tailoring (17.7%). Very few teachers including male & female preferred TV/Radio mechanism (M-9%, F-8.9%) and Domestic wiring (M-10.6%, F-2.5%).

The management variable points out that the majority of the teachers in both the government and private Schools favoured computer courses (M-23.9%, F-29.5%). Most of the teachers working in government management schools favoured Carpentry (17.9%), Book-binding (13.4%), Typewriting (13.4%), Tailoring (11.9%) and the least favoured Domestic wiring (7.5%) whereas the teachers who were working in private management schools favoured Tailoring (20.5%), Book binding (17.9%), Carpentry (12.8%), and the least favoured TV Radio mechanism (6.4%) and Domestic wiring (5.1%).

It is evident that the majority of the teachers from the three regions, male and female teachers working in Government and Private schools expressed that Computer training was suitable and useful to the hearing impaired children because of its demand and more job opportunities.

The Responses of the Teachers Towards the Offering Vocational Education Courses from Various Stages

To know the responses of the teachers towards the offering vocational education courses from various stages, the investigator analysed the collected data with the help the percentage of their responses on the questionnaire and the results obtained are presented in Table 5.7.

It is obvious that the majority of teachers from all the three regions (A-48.2, T-44.1%, R-50%) expressed that they were offering vocational courses from secondary stage, whereas very few teachers of the three regions (A-17.2%, T-17.9%, R-20%) indicated the primary stage (Table 5.7).

Table 5.7: Offering Vocational Education from Various Stages

Sl. No.	Stages	*Regions*			*Gender*		*Management*	
		Coastal Andhra	*Telan-gana*	*Rayala-seema*	*Male*	*Female*	*Govt.*	*Private*
1.	Primary	17.2% (10)	17.9% (12)	20% (4)	15.1% (10)	20.2% (16)	14.9% (10)	20.5% (16)
2.	Upper primary	34.4% (20)	37.4% (25)	30% (6)	39.3% (26)	31.6% (25)	37.3% (25)	32% (25)
3.	Secondary	48.2% (28)	44.7% (30)	50% (10)	45.4% (30)	48.1% (38)	47.7% (32)	47.3% (37)
	Total	**58**	**67**	**20**	**66**	**79**	**67**	**78**

With respect to gender nearly half of the sample i.e. both male (45.4%) and female (48.1%) pointed the secondary stage, whereas very few teachers of both the sexes (M-15.1% F-20.2%) said that it was from the primary stage only. The remaining teachers (M-39.3%, F-31.6%) indicated the upper primary stage.

The management variable shows that more number of teachers working in government schools (47.7%) and private management schools (47.3%) equally stated that they were offering vocational training from the secondary stage, but a few from the both government and private management (G-14.9%, P-20.5%) schools indicated the primary stage.

The Responses of the Teachers Towards onset of Vocational Education

To know the responses of the teachers towards onset of vocational education, the investigator analysed the collected data with the help the percentage of their responses on the questionnaire and the results obtained are presented in Table 5.8 and Fig. 5.2.

Table 5.8 shows that the majority of the teachers from all the three regions of Andhra Pradesh (A-65.5%, T-59.7%, R-65%) expressed that the vocational education training should be started from the upper primary stage, the least number of teachers (A-8.6%, T-10.4%, R-15%) indicated the primary stage.

Table 5.8: Onset of Vocational Education

S. No.	*Stages*	*Regions*			*Gender*		*Management*	
		Coastal Andhra	*Telan-gana*	*Rayala-seema*	*Male*	*Female*	*Govt.*	*Private*
1.	Primary	8.6% (5)	10.4% (7)	15% (3)	15% (10)	6.3% (5)	10.4% (7)	10.2% (8)
2.	Upper primary	65.5% (38)	59.7% (40)	65% (13)	63.6% (42)	62% (49)	64% (43)	61.5% (48)
3.	Secondary	25.8% (15)	29.8% (20)	20% (4)	21.2% (14)	31.6% (25)	25.3% (17)	28.2% (22)
	Total	**58**	**67**	**20**	**66**	**79**	**67**	**78**

With reference to gender both male and female teachers (M-63.6%, F-62%) responded positively in more number for starting vocational training to hearing impaired students at the upper primary stage, whereas very few teachers (M-15%, F-6.3%) indicated the primary stage. On the other teachers from both the Government and Private management schools (G-64%, P-61.5%) expressed that the vocational training should be started from the upper primary stage but very few teachers (G.10.4%, P-10.2%) favoured the primary level.

From the above sources, irrespective of region, gender and type of management, the majority of the teachers opined that the vocational course should be started from the upper primary stage because the early introduction of vocational training would help the special children earn their livelihood at an early age.

The Responses of the Teachers Towards Present Vocational Education Curriculum

To know the responses of the teachers towards present vocational education curriculum, the investigator analysed the collected data with the help the percentage of their responses on the questionnaire and the results obtained are presented in Table 5.9.

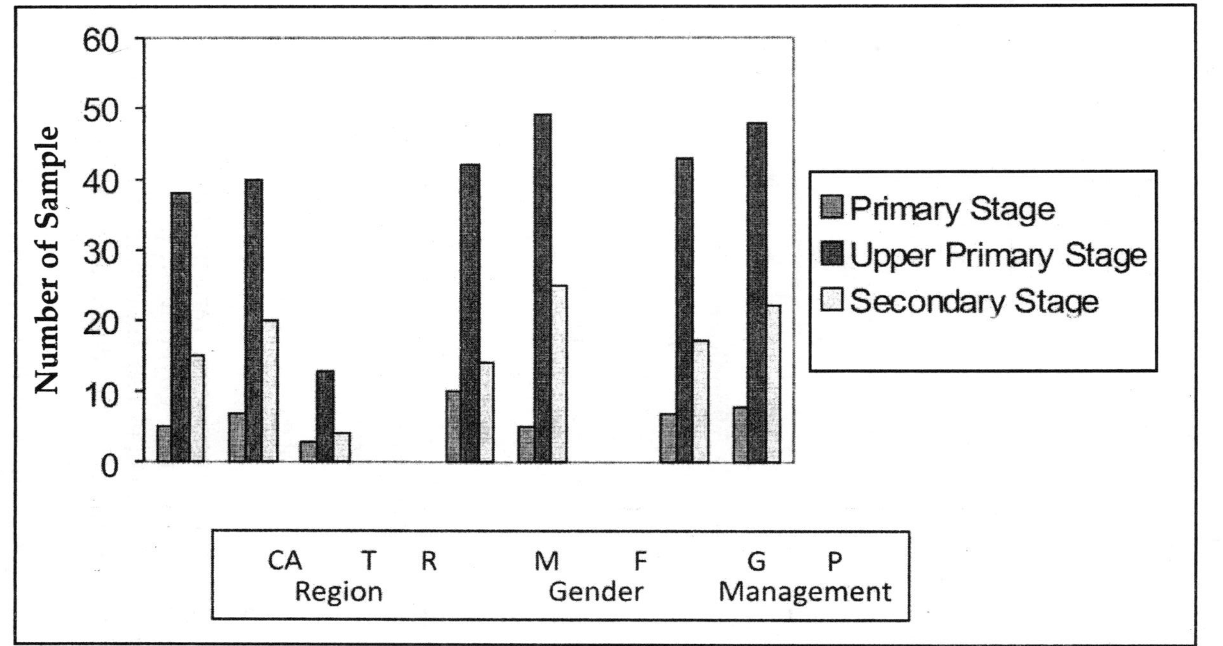

Fig. 5.2: **Offering Vocational Education from various Stages**

Table 5.9: Vocational Education Curriculum

Sl. No.	*Vocational education curriculum framed by*	*Region*			*Gender*		*Management*	
		Coastal Andhra	*Telan-gana*	*Rayala-seema*	*Male*	*Female*	*Govt.*	*Private*
1.	Government prescribed	17.2% (10)	19.4% (13)	20% (4)	13.6% (9)	22.7% (18)	25.3% (17)	12.8% (10)
2.	School designed	25.8% (15)	26.8% (18)	50% (10)	45.4% (21)	27.8% (22)	16.4% (11)	41.1% (32)
3.	No Prescribed Curriculum	56.8% (33)	53.7% (36)	30% (6)	54.5% (36)	49.3% (39)	58.2% (39)	46.1% (36)
	Total	**58**	**67**	**20**	**66**	**79**	**67**	**78**

The data in Table 5.9 indicated that the majority of the teachers (50%) from Rayalaseema region responded that they were following the curriculum designed by their own institutions. Teachers from the Coastal Andhra (25.8%) and Telangana (26.8%) also opined the same. Whereas the teachers from all the three regions (A-56.8%, T-53.7% and R-30%) said that there was no prescribed curriculum for vocational education courses.

The gender variable shows that both the men and women teachers (M-45.4%, F-50.6%) expressed that they were following vocational education curriculum designed by their school. Most of the male and female (M-54.5%, F-49.3%) teachers pointed out that there was no prescribed curriculum for vocational education courses so far.

Considering management variable, the majority of the teachers working under government (58.2%) and private management schools (46.1%) expressed that there was no prescribed curriculum for vocational education courses.

So, it is evident that irrespective of region, gender and type of management, majority of the teachers responded that there was no prescribed curriculum for vocational courses.

This fact supports the finding of Raizada, and Sachetain (1990) which correlated with vocational Education curriculum adopted by the various special schools.

The Responses of the Teachers on Coverage of All Aspects Related to Vocational Education in the Curriculum with Regard to their Region

To know the responses of the teachers on coverage of all aspects related to vocational education in the curriculum with regard to their region, the investigator analysed the collected data with the help of chi-square test and the results obtained are presented in Table 5.10.

Hypothesis

There is no significant difference in the responses of the teachers region wise with regard to the "coverage of all aspects pertaining to vocational education in the curriculum".

Table 5.10: The responses of the teachers on "coverage of all aspects related to vocational education in the curriculum" with regard to their region

Regions in A.P.	*Yes*	*No*	*Total*	χ^2
Coastal Andhra	14	44	58	
Telangana	17	50	67	0.952**
Rayalaseema	7	13	20	
Total	**38**	**107**	**145**	

** Not significant.

The calculated Chi-square value of the responses of the teachers region wise is 0.952 which is less than the table value of 5.991 and not significant at 0.05 level. Therefore, it can be stated that the region of the teachers do not have any significant effect on their responses with regard to the "coverage of all aspects related to vocational education in the curriculum". Hence, it can be said that the formulated hypothesis is retained.

It is evident from Table 5.10 that the majority of the teachers from all the three regions of Andhra Pradesh (107 out of 145) opined that the vocational education curriculum had not covered all aspects.

The Responses of the Teachers on "Coverage of All Aspects Related to Vocational Education in the Curriculum" with Regard to Gender

To know the responses of the teachers on "coverage of all aspects related to vocational education in the curriculum" with regard to gender, the investigator analysed the collected data with the help of chi-square test and the results obtained are presented in Table 5.11.

Hypothesis

There is no significant difference in the expressed responses of the both male and female teachers with respect to the "coverage of all aspects pertaining to vocational education in the curriculum".

Table 5.11: The responses of the teachers on "coverage of all aspects related to vocational education in the curriculum" with regard to gender

Gender	*Yes*	*No*	*Total*	χ^2
Male	15	51	66	
Female	23	56	79	0.464**
Total	**38**	**107**	**145**	

** Not significant.

In Table 5.11 the values of the expressed responses of both the male and female teachers gender wise are distributed and Chi-square values were calculated. The obtained Chi-square values are 0.464 which is less than the table value of 3.841 and not significant at 0.05 levels. Therefore, it is assumed that the gender of the teachers do not have any significant impact on their responses with regard to the "coverage of all aspects pertaining to vocational education in the curriculum". Hence, it can be stated that the formulated hypothesis is retained.

From Table 5.11 it is obvious that both the male and female teachers (107 out of 145) expressed that the "aspects related to vocational education curriculum were not covered".

The Responses of the Teachers Working in Different Management Schools on Coverage of All Aspects Pertaining to Vocational Education in the Curriculum

To know the responses of the teachers working in different management schools on "coverage of all aspects pertaining to vocational education in the curriculum", the investigator analysed the collected data with the help of chi-square test and the results obtained are presented in Table 5.12.

Hypothesis

There is no significant difference in the expressed responses of the teachers with reference to management of the school, in which they are working in the "coverage of all aspects pertaining to vocational education in the curriculum".

Table 5.12: The responses of the teachers working in different management schools on coverage of all aspects pertaining to vocational education in the curriculum

Management	*Yes*	*No*	*Total*	χ^2
Government	12	55	67	
Private	26	52	78	3.67**
Total	**38**	**107**	**145**	

** Not significant.

In Table 5.12 the values of the expressed responses of the teachers working both in Government and private management schools are distributed and Chi-square values were calculated. The Chi-square value 3.67, which is less than the table value of 3.841 and is not significant at 0.05 level. Therefore, it is assumed that the management of school in which they are working does not have significant impact on their responses with reference to the "coverage of all aspects pertaining to vocational education in the curriculum". Hence, it can be said that the formulated hypothesis is retained.

From the above table it is evident that more number of teachers working in both government and private management schools (107 out of 145) opined that the aspects related to vocational education were not covered in the curriculum.

The Responses of the Teachers Towards the Methods of Teaching for Vocational Education

To know the responses of the teachers towards the methods of teaching for vocational education, the investigator analysed the collected data with the help the percentage of their responses on the questionnaire and the results obtained are presented in Table 5.13.

Table 5.13: Responses of the Teachers towards the methods of teaching for vocational education

Sl. No.	*Method of Teaching*	*Region*			*Gender*		*Management*	
		Coastal Andhra	*Telan-gana*	*Rayala-seema*	*Male*	*Female*	*Govt.*	*Private*
1.	Theory Related	31% (18)	22.4% (15)	30% (6)	28.8% (19)	25.3% (20)	31.3% (21)	23.1% (18)
2.	Skill Related	20.6% (12)	23.9% (16)	15% (3)	19.7% (13)	22.8% (18)	23.9% (16)	19.2% (15)
3.	More theory & less skills	48.3% (28)	50.7% (34)	45% (9)	45.4% (30)	51.8% (41)	44.8% (30)	52.6% (41)
4.	More skills & less theory	-	3% (2)	10% (2)	6% (4)	-	-	5.1% (4)
	Total	**58**	**67**	**20**	**66**	**79**	**67**	**78**

It is evident from Table 5.13 that the majority of the teachers from all the three regions of Andhra Prdesh (A-48.3%, T-50.7%, R-45%) expressed that the present vocational education in their schools was imparted with more theory and less skills. The less number of teachers from the Coastal Andhra (31%), Telangana

(22.4%) and Rayalaseema regions (30%) expressed that it was only theory based teaching. A negligible number of teachers from all the three regions (4 out of 145) pointed out it were more skill based with less theory.

With reference to gender variable, both the male (45.5%) and female teachers (51.9%) expressed that the vocational education at present in their schools was more theory based with less skills whereas very less number of male (22.8%) and female teachers (29.7%) indicated it as skill related.

The management variable reveals that the majority of the samples of government (44.8%) and private (52.6%) management schools responded that the present vocational education courses in their institutions were more theory related and less skilled.

It is shown from the above table that all the samples from the three regions, male and female, working in government and private schools expressed that the method of instruction in vocational courses was more theory based with less practical knowledge.

Hence, there is a need to give more importance to skill based instruction in vocational education.

The Responses of the Teachers Towards the Teaching Material to Teach Vocational Education Courses

To know the responses of the teachers towards the teaching material to teach vocational education courses, the investigator analysed the collected data with the help the percentage of their responses on the questionnaire and the results obtained are presented in Table 5.14.

Table 5.14 shows the responses of the Coastal Andhra and Telangana (A-65.5%, T-73.1%) teachers in respect of utilising any separate teaching material to teach vocational education courses, were negative whereas the Rayalaseema (80%) teachers expressed that they were using the separate teaching material designed by the institutions.

Table 5.14: Responses of the Teachers towards the teaching material to teach vocational education courses

Teaching method	*Region*			*Gender*		*Management*	
	Coastal Andhra	*Telan-gana*	*Rayala-seema*	*Male*	*Female*	*Govt.*	*Private*
Yes	34.4% (20)	26.8% (18)	80% (16)	42.4% (28)	32.9% (26)	44.8% (30)	30.8% (24)
No	65.5% (38)	73.1% (49)	20% (4)	57.5% (38)	67% (53)	55.2% (37)	69.2% (54)
Total	**58**	**67**	**20**	**66**	**79**	**67**	**78**

The gender variable pointed out that both the men and women teachers (M-57.5%, W-67%) responded that they were not using any separate teaching material to teach vocational educational courses.

The management variable reveals that more number of private management school teachers (69.2%) were not utilising teaching material to teach vocational courses, whereas 58.2% of government school teachers expressed similar opinion.

This needs a special attention to provide the appropriate teaching learning material to teach vocational courses more effectively.

Responses of the Teachers Towards Their Training Qualifications

To know the responses of the teachers towards their training qualifications, the investigator analysed the collected data with the help the percentage of their responses on the questionnaire and the results obtained are presented in Table 5.15.

Table 5.15 shows that nearly half of the teachers from all the three regions (A-51.7%, T-55.2%, R-60%) expressed that vocational trained teachers were teaching vocational courses, whereas the teachers from all the three regions (A-48.2%, T-44.7%, R-40%) responded that general trained teachers were also teaching the same courses.

Table 5.15: Responses of the Teachers towards their training qualifications

S. No.	*Vocational Educational Courses*	*Region*			*Gender*		*Management*	
		Coastal Andhra	*Telan-gana*	*Rayala-seema*	*Male*	*Female*	*Govt.*	*Private*
1.	Vocational trained teachers	51.7% (30)	55.2% (37)	60% (12)	54.5% (36)	54.4% (43)	55.2% (37)	53.8% (42)
2.	General trained teachers	48.2% (28)	44.7% (30)	40% (8)	45.5% (30)	45.5% (36)	44.7% (30)	46.1% (36)
	Total	**58**	**67**	**20**	**66**	**79**	**67**	**78**

Genderwise both male and female teachers (M-54.5%, F-54.4%) equally expressed that vocational trained teachers were teaching vocational courses.

With regard to the type of management teachers in government and private management schools (G-55.2%, P-53.8%) expressed that the vocational trained teachers were teaching vocational courses.

Regionwise Responses of the Teachers with Regard to Sufficient Working Hours Allotted for Vocational Course

To know the region wise responses of the teachers with regard to sufficient working hours allotted for vocational course, the investigator analysed the collected data with the help of chi-square test and the results obtained are presented in Table 5.16.

Hypothesis

There is no significant difference in the responses of the teachers region wise with respect to the "Sufficient Working hours allotted for Vocational Courses".

Table 5.16: The region wise responses of the teachers with regard to sufficient working hours allotted for vocational course

Regions in A.P.	*Yes*	*No*	*Total*	χ^2
Coastal Andhra	13	45	58	
Telangana	13	54	67	0.348**
Rayalaseema	5	15	20	
Total	**31**	**114**	**145**	

** Not significant.

It is observed from the above table that the calculated Chi-square value of the responses of the teachers region wise is 0.348 which is less than the table value 5.991 and not significant at 0.05 level. Therefore, it can be stated that the region of teachers do not have any significant value on their responses with respect to the sufficient working hours allotted for vocational courses. Hence it can be said that the formulated hypothesis is retained.

Majority of the teachers from all the three regions (114 out of 145) stated that the allotment of working hours for vocational training was not sufficient. Only 31 out of 145 teachers expressed that the allotted working hours for vocational courses were sufficient.

Responses of Male and Female Teachers on Allotment of Insufficient Working Hours for Vocational Courses

To know the responses of male and female teachers on allotment of insufficient working hours for vocational courses, the investigator analysed the collected data with the help of chi-square test and the results obtained are presented in Table 5.17.

Hypothesis

There is no significant difference in the responses of the both male and female teachers with regard to the "Allotment of Sufficient Working Hours for Vocational Courses".

Table 5.17: Responses of male and female teachers on allotment of insufficient working hours for vocational courses

Gender	*Yes*	*No*	*Total*	χ^2
Male	13	53	66	
Female	18	61	79	0.616**
Total	**31**	**114**	**145**	

** Not significant.

The values of the responses of the both male and female teachers the Table 5.2 distributed and Chi-square values were calculated. The Chi-square value is 0.616, which is less than table value of 3.841 and not significant at 0.05 level. Therefore, it is opined that the responses of both male and female teachers do not have any significant impact on their responses with regard to the "allotment of sufficient working hours for vocational courses (are sufficient). Hence it can be asserted that the formulated hypothesis is accepted.

With reference to gender variable, both the male and female teachers (114 out of 145) responded that the allotted working hours for vocational training were not sufficient. Whereas only 31 out of 145 stated that the allotted working hours for vocational courses were sufficient.

Responses of the Teachers Genderwise on Allotment of Sufficient Working Hours for Vocational Courses

To know the responses of the teachers gender wise on allotment of sufficient working hours for vocational courses, the investigator analysed the collected data with the help of chi-square test and the results obtained are presented in Table 5.18.

Hypothesis

There is no significant difference in the responses of the teachers in relation to the type of management in with they are working with respect to the "allotment of sufficient working hours for vocational courses".

Table 5.18: Responses of the teachers gender wise on the "Allotment of Sufficient Working hours for Vocational Courses"

Management	*Yes*	*No*	*Total*	χ^2
Government	15	52	67	
Private	16	62	78	0.051**
Total	**31**	**114**	**145**	

** Not significant.

In Table 5.18 the values of the responses of the both male and female teachers are distributed and found that Chi-square value is 0.051 which is less than the table value of 3.841 and not significant at 0.05 level. Therefore, it is stated that the responses of the teachers working both in government and private management schools do not have any significant impact on their responses with reference to allotment of working hours for vocational courses.

From the above table it is evident that the majority of the teachers working in government (52 out of 67) and private (62 out of 78) management schools expressed that the allotment of working hours for vocational training classes was not sufficient whereas very few teachers (31 out of 145) opined contrarily.

Responses of the Teachers Towards Vocational Education Examination Pattern

To know the responses of the teachers towards vocational education examination pattern, the investigator analysed the collected data with the help the percentage of their responses on the questionnaire and the results obtained are presented in Table 5.19 and Fig. 5.3.

FromTable 5.19 it is obvious that the majority of the teachers from the three regions of Andhra Pradesh i.e. Coastal Andhra (79.3%), Telangana (73.1%) and Rayalaseema (45%) revealed that they were not conducting any vocational examinations in their schools, whereas the remaining teachers said that they were holding along with the general examinations (CA-15.2%, T-16.4%, R-30%). But a few teachers expressed that (CA-5.2%, T10.4%, R-25%) they were conducting vocational examinations separately.

Table 5.19: Vocational Education Examination Pattern

Sl. No	*Procedure*	*Regions*			*Gender*		*Management*	
		Coastal Andhra	*Telan-gana*	*Rayala-seema*	*Male*	*Female*	*Govt.*	*Private*
1.	Along with general exams	15.5% (9)	16.4% (11)	30% (6)	18.1% (12)	17.7% (14)	19.4% (13)	16.6% (13)
2.	Separate exam	5.2% (3)	10.4% (7)	25% (5)	7.5% (5)	12.6% (10)	-	19.2% (15)
3.	No exams	79.3% (46)	73.1% (49)	45% (9)	74.2% (49)	69.6% (55)	80.5% (54)	64% (50)
	Total	**58**	**67**	**20**	**66**	**79**	**67**	**78**

The gender variable shows that both the men (74.2%) and women (69.6%) teachers pointed out that they were not conducting any vocational examination. Whereas men teachers (18.1%) and women teachers (17.7%) expressed that they were doing along with the general examinations. But only a few men (7.5%) and women (12.6%) teachers responded that they were conducting vocational educational examinations separately.

The management variable shows that the teachers from both the government (80.5%) and private (64%) management schools expressed that they were not conducting any vocational education examination separately. Whereas a few teachers from the government (19.4%) and Private (16.6%) schools indicated that they were doing along with the general examination. But only the teachers of private management schools (19.2%) revealed that they were conducting vocational education examination separately.

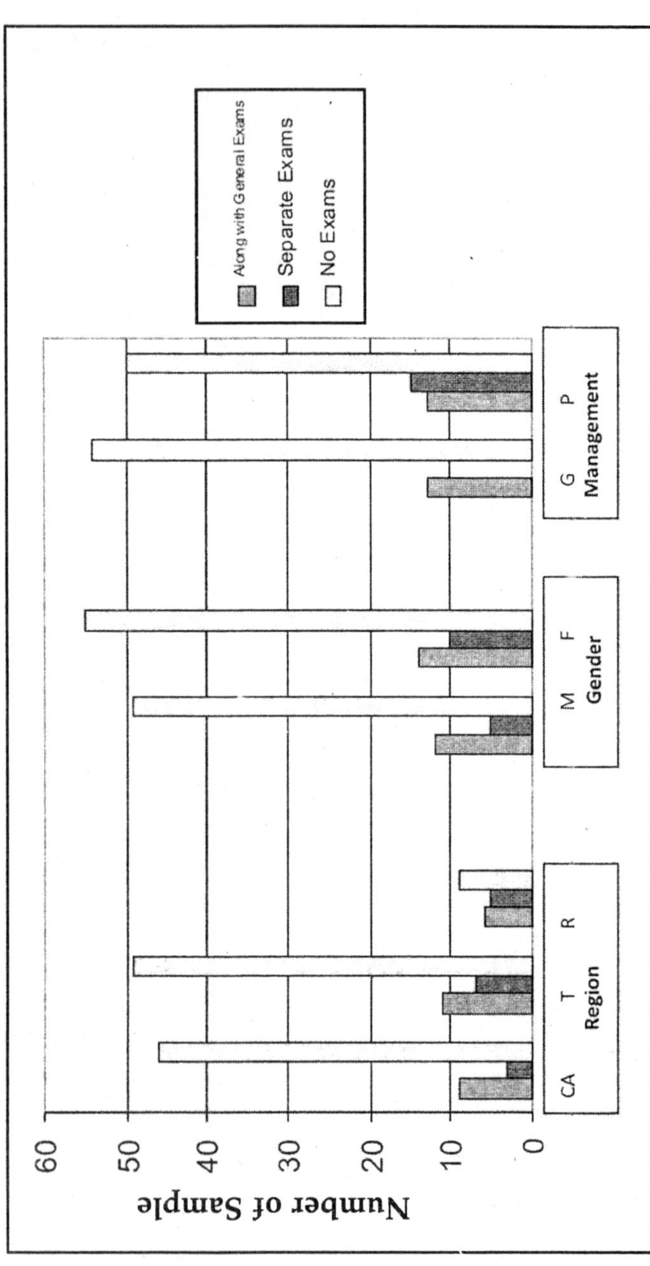

Fig. 5.3: **Conducting of Vocational Education Examinations**

Responses of the Teachers Towards Vocational Education Examination Pattern

To know the responses of the teachers towards vocational education examination pattern, the investigator analysed the collected data with the help the percentage of their responses on the questionnaire and the results obtained are presented in Table 5.20.

Table 5.20: Vocational Education Evaluation Procedure

S. No	Test procedure	*Regions*			*Gender*		*Management*	
		Coastal Andhra	*Telan-gana*	*Rayala-seema*	*Male*	*Female*	*Govt.*	*Private*
1.	Theory Based	8.6% (5)	5.9% (4)	10% (2)	9% (6)	6.3% (5)	5.9% (4)	8.9% (7)
2.	Practical Based	8.6% (5)	8.9% (6)	10% (2)	13.6% (9)	5% (4)	7.4% (5)	10.2% (8)
3.	Both theory & practical	17.2% (10)	20.8% (14)	50% (10)	33.3% (22)	18.2% (12)	14.9% (10)	30.8% (24)
4.	None of these	65.5% (38)	64.1% (43)	30% (6)	43.9% (29)	87.8% (58)	71.6% (48)	50% (39)
	Total	**58**	**67**	**20**	**66**	**79**	**67**	**78**

The data in Table 5.20 reveal that more number of teachers from the three regions expressed that there was no specific test procedure for vocational education courses i.e. Coastal Andhra (65.5%), Telangana (64.1%) and Rayalaseema (30%), whereas a few teachers pointed out theory based vocational education test (CA-8.6%, T-5.9%, R-10%) and practical based test procedure (CA-8.6%, T.8.9%, R-10%). Among the three regions Rayalaaseema teachers (50%) said that they were following both theory and practical based vocational tests.

With respect to gender, the majority of the women teachers (87.8%) expressed that there was no specific vocational education test procedure whereas very few teachers (M-9%, F-6.3%) responded that there was theory based test and practical based test (M-13.6% and F-5%). In relation to both practical and theory only men teachers (33.3%) responded positively.

Considering the type of management of the school in which the teachers were working, they expressed that they were evaluating both i.e. theory based and practical based evaluation.

Responses of the Teachers Towards Vocational Education Examination Pattern

To know the responses of the teachers towards vocational education examination pattern, the investigator analysed the collected data with the help the percentage of their responses on the questionnaire and the results obtained are presented in Table 5.21.

Table 5.21: How to Conduct Vocational Education Examinations

S. No.	*Vocational Educational Courses*	*Region*			*Gender*		*Management*	
		Coastal Andhra	*Telan-gana*	*Rayala-seema*	*Male*	*Female*	*Govt.*	*Private*
1.	Along with general	43.1% (25)	29.9% (20)	20% (4)	40.9% (27)	27.8% (22)	43.2% (29)	25.6% (20)
2.	Separate	56.8% (33)	70% (47)	80% (16)	59% (39)	72.1% (57)	56.7% (38)	74.4% (58)
	Total	58	67	20	66	79	67	78

Table 5.21 shows that most of the teachers from the three regions of Andhra Pradesh i.e. Coastal Andhra (56.8%), Telangana (70%) and Rayalaseema (80%) said that it was better to conduct vocational education examinations separately. Whereas the teachers from the Coastal Andhra (43.1%), Telangana (29.9%) and Rayalaseema (20%) indicated that the vocational education examinations should be conducted along with the general education.

The gender variable pointed out that the men teachers (59%) and women teachers (72.1%) were in favour of conducting separate vocational education examinations, whereas 40.9% of men teachers and 27.8% of women teachers opined that it should be done along with the general education.

Considering management variable, the majority of the private management school teachers (74.4%) and teachers of government schools (55.2%) expressed vocational examinations should be conducted separately. About 43.2% of teachers working in government schools and 25.6% of private school teachers expressed that the vocational education examinations should be conducted along with the general education.

Responses of the Teachers Towards Vocational Education Examination Pattern

To know the responses of the teachers towards vocational education examination pattern, the investigator analysed the collected data with the help of chi-square test and the results obtained are presented in Table 5.22.

Hypothesis

There is no significant difference in the region wise expressed responses of the teachers on "Minimum pass marks in vocational education courses".

Table 5.22: Region wise responses of teachers on "minimum pass marks in vocational education courses"

Regions in A.P.	*Yes*	*No*	*Total*	χ^2
Coastal Andhra	11	47	58	0.0239**
Telangana	13	54	67	
Rayalaseema	4	16	20	
Total	**28**	**117**	**145**	

** Not significant.

It is observed from Table 5.22 that the calculated Chi-square value of the responses of the region wise teachers is 0.0239 which is less than the table value of 5.991 and is not significant at 0.05 level. Therefore, it can be stated that the Region of the teachers does not have any significant value on their responses with regard to "minimum pass marks in vocational education courses". Hence, it is said that the formulated hypothesis is retained.

From the above table it is evident that the majority of the teachers from all the three regions (117 out of 145) responded that the minimum pass marks need not be considered for promotion of vocational education as equivalent to normal, whereas only 28 out of 145 teachers turned it.

Responses of the Teachers Towards Vocational Education Examination Pattern

To know the responses of the teachers towards vocational education examination pattern, the investigator analysed the collected data with the help of chi-square test and the results obtained are presented in Table 5.23.

Hypothesis

There is no significant difference in the responses of both male and female teachers with regard to "minimum pass marks in vocational education courses".

Table 5.23: Genderwise the responses of the teachers on "minimum pass marks in vocational education courses"

Gender	*Yes*	*No*	*Total*	χ^2
Boys	56	10	66	
Girls	61	18	79	0.899**
Total	**117**	**28**	**145**	

** Not significant.

It is evident from Table 5.23 that the calculated Chi-square value of the responses of the gender wise teachers is 0.899 which is less than the table value of 3.841 and is not significant at 0.05 level. Therefore, it is observed that the gender of the teachers does not have any significant value on their responses with regard to "minimum pass marks in vocational education courses". Hence, it can be stated that the formulated hypothesis is accepted.

It is evident from the above table that both male and female teachers (117 out of 145) opined that there should not be minimum pass marks for vocational courses just like normal. Only some teachers (28 out of 145) stated that there should be minimum pass marks for vocational students just as normal students.

Responses of the Teachers Towards Vocational Education Examination Pattern

To know the responses of the teachers towards vocational education examination pattern, the investigator analysed the collected data with the help of chi-square test and the results obtained are presented in Table 5.24.

Hypothesis

There is no significant difference in the responses of the teachers in relation to type of management of school in which they are working with regard to "minimum pass marks in vocational education courses".

Table 5.24: The responses of teachers in relation to management of school on "minimum pass marks in vocational education courses"

Management	*Yes*	*No*	*Total*	χ^2
Government	54	13	67	0.034**
Private	63	15	78	
Total	**117**	**28**	**145**	

** Not significant

It is observed from Table 5.24 that the calculated Chi-square value of the responses of the teachers working both government and private management schools is 0.034 which is less than the table value of 3.841 and is not significant at 0.05 level. Therefore it can be stated that the type of management of schools in which the teachers are working does not have any significant value on their responses with regard to minimum pass marks in vocational education courses. Hence it is stated that the formulated hypothesis is retained.

It is observed can be seen from the above table that the majority of the teachers (117 out of 145) working in government as well as in private schools expressed that there should not be minimum pass marks for promotion of vocational training students just like normal students. Whereas less very few teachers (28 out of 145) opined its positively.

Responses of the Teachers Towards Vocational Education Examination Pattern

To know the responses of the teachers towards vocational education examination pattern, the investigator analysed the collected data with the help of chi-square test and the results obtained are presented in Table 5.25.

Hypothesis

There is no significant difference in the responses of the teachers of the three regions on the "Issue of Vocational Education course certificates to the hearing impaired students".

Table 5.25: The responses of the teachers region wise on the "issue of vocational education course certificates to the students"

Regions in A.P.	*Yes*	*No*	*Total*	χ^2
Coastal Andhra	20	38	58	1.10**
Telangana	18	49	67	
Rayalaseema	5	15	20	
Total	**43**	**102**	**145**	

** Not Significant.

In Table 5.25 the values of the expressed responses of the teachers of three regions are distributed and Chi-square values are calculated. The chi-square values 1.10 is less than the table value of 9.21 and is not significant at 0.01 level. Therefore, it is assumed that the region of the teachers does not have any significant impact on their responses with respect to the "Issue of Vocational Education course certificate to the students." Hence, it can be said that the formulated hypothesis is retained.

Responses of the Teachers Towards Vocational Education Examination Pattern

To know the responses of the teachers towards vocational education examination pattern, the investigator analysed the collected data with the help of chi-square test and the results obtained are presented in Table 5.26.

Hypothesis

There is no significant difference in the responses of the both male and female teachers with respect to Gender on the "Issue of Vocational Education Course Certificate" to the Hearing Impaired Students.

Table 5.26: The gender wise responses of the teachers on the "issue of vocational education course certificate to the students"

Gender	*Yes*	*No*	*Total*	χ^2
Male	20	46	66	
Female	23	56	79	0.0007**
Total	**43**	**102**	**145**	

** Not Significant.

In Table 5.26 the values of the responses of the male and female teachers are distributed and chi-square values were calculated. The obtained Chi-square value 0.0007 is less than the table value of 5.991 and not significant at 0.05 level. Therefore, it is assumed that the gender of the teachers do not have any significant effect on their responses with reference to the "Issue of Vocational Education Course Certificates to the students". Hence, it can be stated that the formulated hypothesis is retained.

Responses of the Teachers Towards Vocational Education Examination Pattern

To know the responses of the teachers towards vocational education examination pattern, the investigator analysed the collected data with the help of chi-square test and the results obtained are presented in Table 5.27.

Hypothesis

There is no significant difference in the expressed responses of the teachers in relation to the type of management of the school in which they are working on the "Issue of Vocational Education Course Certificates to the students".

Table 5.27: The responses of the teachers with respect to management of the school, on the "Issue of Vocational Education Course Certificate to the students"

Management	*Yes*	*No*	*Total*	χ^2
Government	23	44	67	
Private	20	58	78	0.920**
Total	**43**	**102**	**145**	

** Not Significant.

In Table 5.27 the values of the responses of the teachers working in different management schools are distributed and Chi-square values were calculated. The Chi-square value 0.920 is less than the table value of 5.991 and not significant at 0.05 level. Therefore, it is assumed that the management of school in which the teachers are working does not have significant impact on their responses with reference to the "Issue of Vocational Education course certificates to the students. Hence, it can be stated that the formulated hypothesis is retained.

Responses of the Teachers Towards Vocational Education Examination Pattern

To know the responses of the teachers towards vocational education examination pattern, the investigator analysed the collected data with the help of chi-square test and the results obtained are presented in Table 5.28.

Table 5.28: The region wise responses of the teachers on the "Usefulness of Vocational Education Certificates in Getting Jobs"

Regions in A.P.	*Yes*	*No*	*Total*	χ^2
Coastal Andhra	20	38	58	
Telangana	28	39	67	0.719**
Rayalaseema	8	12	20	
Total	**56**	**89**	**145**	

** Not significant.

Hypothesis

There is no significant difference in the responses of the teachers with respect to region on the "usefulness of vocational education certificates in getting jobs".

In Table 5.28 responses of the teachers from the three regions are distributed and Chi-square values were calculated. The obtained Chi-square value is 0.719 which is less than the table value of 5.991 and not significant at 0.05 level. Therefore it can be stated that the region of the teachers do not have any significant value on their responses with regard to the "usefulness of the vocational education certificate in getting jobs". Hence, it is stated that the formulated hypothesis is retained.

From the above table it is evident that more number of teachers (89 out of 145) from all the three regions opined that the vocational education certificates were not useful in securing jobs. Whereas some teachers (56 out of 145) responded that the vocational education courses certificates were not useful for securing jobs.

Responses of the Teachers Towards Vocational Education Examination Pattern

To know the responses of the teachers towards vocational education examination pattern, the investigator analysed the collected data with the help of chi-square test and the results obtained are presented in Table 5.29.

Table 5.29: Genderwise responses of the teachers on the "usefulness of vocational education certificates in getting jobs"

Gender	*Yes*	*No*	*Total*	χ^2
Male	24	42	66	
Female	32	47	79	0.114**
Total	**56**	**89**	**145**	

** Not significant.

Hypothesis

There is no significant difference in the gender wise responses of the teachers with respect to the "usefulness of Vocational Education Certificate in getting jobs".

In Table 5.29 the values of the responses of both the male and female teachers are distributed and the Chi-square values were calculated. The obtained chi-square value 0.114 is less than the table value of 3.841 and not significant at 0.05 level. Therefore it is observed that the gender of the teachers does not have any significant effect on their responses with regard to the "usefulness of vocational education certificates in getting jobs". Hence it is stated that the formulated hypothesis is retained.

From the above table it is evident that the majority of the male teachers (42 out of 66) and female teachers (47 out of 79) irrespective of their gender opined that the vocational education course certificates offered were not keeping the students in advantageous position compared to the others in taking up jobs. Very few male teachers (24 out of 66) and female teachers (32 out of 79) responded that the vocational education certificate might help them in getting jobs.

Responses of the Teachers Towards Vocational Education Examination Pattern

To know the responses of the teachers towards vocational education examination pattern, the investigator analysed the collected data with the help of chi-square test and the results obtained are presented in Table 5.30.

Hypothesis

There is no significant difference in the responses of the teachers in relation to management of the school on the "usefulness of vocational education certificates in getting jobs".

Table 5.30: Responses of the teachers in relation to management of the school on the "usefulness of certificates in getting jobs"

Management	*Vocational Trained*	*General quality*	*Total*	χ^2
Government	23	44	67	
Private	33	45	78	0.660**
Total	**56**	**89**	**145**	

** Not significant.

In Table 5.30 the values of the expressed of the teachers working in different management schools are distributed and the Chi-square values were calculated. The obtained Chi-square value 0.660 is less than the table value of 3.841 and is not significant at 0.05 level. Therefore, it is assumed that the management of the schools in which the teachers are working does not have any significant impact on their responses with respect to the "usefulness of vocational education certificates in getting Jobs." Hence, it can be stated that the formulated hypothesis is accepted.

From the above table it evident that majority of the teachers working in government schools (44 out of 67) and private schools (45 out of 78) stated that there was no utility with the vocational educational certificate in securing jobs. Only a less number of government teachers (23 out of 67) and private school teachers (33 out of 78) responded positively.

Responses of the Teachers Towards Vocational Education Examination Pattern

To know the responses of the teachers towards vocational education examination pattern, the investigator analysed the collected data with the help of chi-square test and the results obtained are presented in Table 5.31.

Table 5.31: Attending In-service Training Programmes

Sl. No.	*Attending in-service vocational training programmes*	*Region*			*Gender*		*Management*	
		Coastal Andhra	*Telan-gana*	*Rayala-seema*	*Male*	*Female*	*Govt.*	*Private*
1.	Yes	34.4% (20)	40.3% (27)	75% (15)	60.6% (40)	21.5% (17)	37.3% (25)	41% (32)
2.	No	65.5% (38)	59.7% (40)	25% (5)	39.3% (26)	78.4% (62)	62.6% (42)	58.9% (46)
	Total	**58**	**67**	**20**	**66**	**79**	**67**	**78**

From the above Table 5.31 it is obvious that the majority of the teachers from the Coastal Andhra (65.5%) and Telangana (59.7%) pointed out that they were not attending in-service training programmes. In contrast more number of Rayalaseema teachers (75%) responded positively.

With reference to gender variable, when compared to the male teachers (39.3%) more number of women teachers (78.4%) indicated that they were not attending in service training programmes whereas more number of male teachers (60.6%) spoke positively because men teachers had more access and interest to attend vocational training programmes than women teachers.

Considering management variable, teachers working in both the government and private management schools (G-62.6%, P-58.9%) expressed that they were not attending in-service training programmes, whereas when compared to teachers working in government schools, (37.3%) more number of teachers from private management schools (41%) responded positively.

This finding supports the finding of Swain (1992) which correlates with the finding that, there is no provision for in-service training programmes.

Responses of the Teachers Towards Vocational Education Examination Pattern

To know the responses of the teachers towards vocational education examination pattern, the investigator analysed the collected data with the help of chi-square test and the results obtained are presented in Table 5.32.

Hypothesis

There is no significant difference in the responses of the teachers of the three regions with regard to "training programmes in vocational education are useful".

Table 5.32: The region wise responses of the teachers on "training programmes in vocational education are useful"

Regions in A.P.	*Yes*	*No*	*Total*	χ^2
Coastal Andhra	46	12	58	
Telangana	47	20	67	1.376**
Rayalaseema	15	5	20	
Total	**108**	**37**	**145**	

** Not significant.

It is observed from Table 5.32 that the values of the expressed responses of the teachers of three regions are distributed and Chi-square values were calculated. The obtained

Chi-square value 1.376 is less than the table value of 5.991 and is not significant at 0.05 level. Therefore, it is assumed that the region of the teachers have no significant value on their responses on usefulness of training programmes in vocational education. Hence it can be said that the formulated hypothesis is accepted.

From the above table it is evident that majority of the teachers from all the three regions (108 out of 145) have responded that training programmes in vocational education are useful to them. Only some teachers (37 out of 145) have opined that the vocational training programmes are not useful.

Responses of the Teachers Towards Vocational Education Examination Pattern

To know the responses of the teachers towards vocational education examination pattern, the investigator analysed the collected data with the help of chi-square test and the results obtained are presented in Table 5.33.

Hypothesis

There is no significant difference in the gender wise responses of the teachers with regard to the "training programmes in vocational education are useful".

Table 5.33: Genderwise responses of the teachers on "usefulness of attending training programmes in vocational education"

Gender	*Yes*	*No*	*Total*	χ^2
Male	53	13	66	
Female	55	24	79	1.633**
Total	108	37	145	

** Not significant.

It is evident from Table 5.33 that the values of the responses of both male and female teachers are distributed and the chi-square values were calculated. The obtained Chi-square value is

1.633 which is less than the table value of 3.841 and is not significant at 0.05 level. Therefore, it is assumed that the gender of the teachers have no significant value on their responses on "training programmes in vocational education are useful". Hence, it can be stated that the formulated hypothesis is retained.

From the above table it is obvious that the majority of the male teachers (53 out of 66) and female teachers (55 out of 79) responded that the vocational education training programmes were useful whereas only a small number of male teachers (13 out of 66) and female teachers (24 out of 79) neglected it.

Responses of the Teachers Towards Vocational Education Examination Pattern

To know the responses of the teachers towards vocational education examination pattern, the investigator analysed the collected data with the help of chi-square test and the results obtained are presented in Table 5.34.

Hypothesis

There is no significant difference in the responses of the teachers in relation to type of management of the school in which they are working on "training programmes in vocational education are useful".

Table 5.34: Responses of the teachers of different management of the schools on "usefulness of training programmes"

Management	*Yes*	*No*	*Total*	χ^2
Government	53	14	67	
Private	55	23	78	0.984**
Total	**108**	**37**	**145**	

** Not significant.

It is evident from Table 5.34 that the values of the responses of the teachers in both government and private management schools are distributed and the Chi-square values were calculated. The Chi-square value 0.984 which is less than the table value of 3.841 and not significant at 0.05 level. Therefore, it is assumed that the category of teachers of both government and private management schools do not have any significant impact on their responses with regard to "Training programmes in vocational education are useful". Hence it can be said that the formulated hypothesis is retained.

The data from the above table that more number of government school teachers (53 out of 67) and private school teachers (55 out of 78) opined that the vocational education training programmes were useful. Surprisingly very less number of government school teachers (14 out of 67) and private school teachers (23 out of 78) spoke in a negative way.

Responses of the Teachers Towards Vocational Education Examination Pattern

To know the responses of the teachers towards vocational education examination pattern, the investigator analysed the collected data with the help of chi-square test and the results obtained are presented in Table 5.35.

Hypothesis

There is no significant difference in the region wise responses of teachers with respect to the "receipt of financial assistance to conduct vocational education courses is adequate".

Table 5.35: Indicates the region wise responses of the teachers on "the receipt of financial assistance"

Regions in A.P.	*Yes*	*No*	*Total*	χ^2
Coastal Andhra	10	48	56	
Telangana	12	55	67	0.632**
Rayalaseema	5	15	20	
Total	**27**	**118**	**145**	

** Not significant.

It is observed from Table 5.35 that the values of the region wise responses of the teachers region wise are distributed and Chi-square values were calculated. The chi-square value is 0.632 which is less than the table value 3.841 and is not significant at 0.05 level. Therefore it is assumed that the region of the teachers does not have any significant impact on their responses with regard to the adequacy of financial assistance received to conduct vocational educational courses. Hence it is stated that the formulated hypothesis is accepted.

From the above table it is observed that the majority of the teachers from all the three regions (118 out of 145) opined that the receipt of financial assistance was not adequate. Only a few teachers 27 out of 145 stated surprisingly that the receipt of financial assistance was adequate.

Responses of the Teachers Towards Vocational Education Examination Pattern

To know the responses of the teachers towards vocational education examination pattern, the investigator analysed the collected data with the help of chi-square test and the results obtained are presented in Table 5.36.

Hypothesis

There is no significant difference in the gender wise responses of the teachers with regard to the "adequacy of financial assistance to conduct vocational education courses".

Table 5.36: Gender wise responses of the teachers on the adequacy of financial assistance received

Gender	*Yes*	*No*	*Total*	χ^2
Male	12	54	66	
Female	15	64	79	0.081**
Total	**27**	**118**	**145**	

** Not significant.

It is obvious from Table 5.36 that the values of the expressed responses of the teachers with regard to gender wise are distributed and Chi-square values were calculated. The Chi-square value 0.0891is less than the table value of 3.841 and not significant at 0.05 level. Therefore, it is assumed that the region of the teachers does not have any significant impact on the adequacy of financial assistance they received to conduct vocational education courses. Hence, it is observed that the formulated hypothesis is retained.

From the above table it is clear that the majority of the teachers (118 out of 145) with respect to gender stated that the receipt of financial assistance was not adequate. Surprisingly only a few, 27 out of 145 gave negative opinion.

Responses of the Teachers Towards Vocational Educational Examination Pattern

To know the responses of the teachers towards vocational education examination pattern, the investigator analysed the collected data with the help of chi-square test and the results obtained are presented in Table 5.37.

Hypothesis

There is no significant difference in the responses of the teachers in relation to the type of management of the school in which they are working "to conduct vocational education courses the receipt of financial assistance is adequate".

Table 5.37: Responses of the teachers in relation to type of management the "receipt of financial assistance"

Management	*Yes*	*No*	*Total*	χ^2
Government	10	57	67	0.714**
Private	17	61	78	
Total	**27**	**118**	**145**	

** Not significant.

From the above Table 5.37 it is obvious that the values of the responses of the teachers of both government and private management schools are distributed and Chi-square values were calculated. The Chi-square value 0.714 is less than the table value of 3.84 and is not significant at 0.05 level. Therefore it is assumed that there is no significant impact of different management school "on the adequacy of financial assistance" they have been receiving to conduct vocational education course. Hence, it can be said that the formulated hypothesis is rejected.

The management variable shows that the majority of the teacher 118 out of 145 working in both government and private schools opined that the receipt of financial assistance was not adequate.

It shows that there is need to provide adequate financial assistance to conduct/run vocational courses.

RESPONSES OF THE TEACHERS TOWARDS VOCATIONAL EDUCATION EXAMINATION PATTERN

To know the responses of the teachers towards vocational education examination pattern, the investigator analysed the collected data with the help the percentage of their responses on the questionnaire and the results obtained are presented in Table 5.38 and Fig. 5.4.

Table 5.38 depicts that more number of teachers from all the three regions of Andhra Pradesh i.e. Coastal Andhra (34.4%), Telangana (32.8%) and Rayalaseema (30%) expressed that there was no relationship between general education and vocational education courses. The least number of teachers of Coastal Andhra (8.6%), Telangana (7.4%) and Rayalaseema (30%) responded that there was no sufficient time for vocational courses. Whereas the other responses wise as follows non-saleable vocational education (CA-27.5%, T-29.8%, R-25%) and inadequate infrastructure facilities (CA-29.3%, T-29.8%, R-30%).

Table 5.38: Problems in Relation to Vocational Education

Sl. No.	*Problems related to vocational education*	*Region*			*Gender*		*Management*	
		Coastal Andhra	*Telan-gana*	*Rayala-seema*	*Male*	*Female*	*Govt.*	*Private*
1.	Non-Saleble Vocational Education	27.5% (16)	29.8% (20)	25% (5)	34.8% (23)	22.7% (18)	35.8% (24)	21.7% (17)
2.	No Relationship between general & Vocational Education	34.4% (20)	32.8% (22)	30% (6)	33.3% (22)	32.9% (26)	29.8% (20)	35.8% (28)
3.	Inadequate infrastructure facilities	29.3% (17)	29.8% (20)	30% (6)	27.3% (18)	31.6% (25)	29.8% (20)	29.4% (23)
4.	Insufficient Time	8.6% (5)	7.4% (5)	15% (3)	4.5% (3)	12.6% (10)	4.4% (3)	12.8% (10)
	Total	**58**	**67**	**20**	**66**	**79**	**67**	**78**

With reference to the gender variable, when compared to the female sample, more number of male samples expressed that the problems faced in vocational education were non-saleable of vocational education (M-34.8%, F-22.7%) and there was no relationship between general education and vocational education (M-33.3%, F-32.9%) whereas more number of female teachers (12.6%) compared to male teachers (5.1%) said that the time allotted for vocational education was not sufficient. But surprisingly both male (27.3%) and female (31.6%) respondents expressed that the problems related to vocational education were due to lack of infrastructure facilities.

The management variable points out that both the government and private management samples equally (G-29.8, P-29.4%) expressed that the main problem in vocational education was insufficient infrastructure facilities. When compared to the private schools number of government teachers

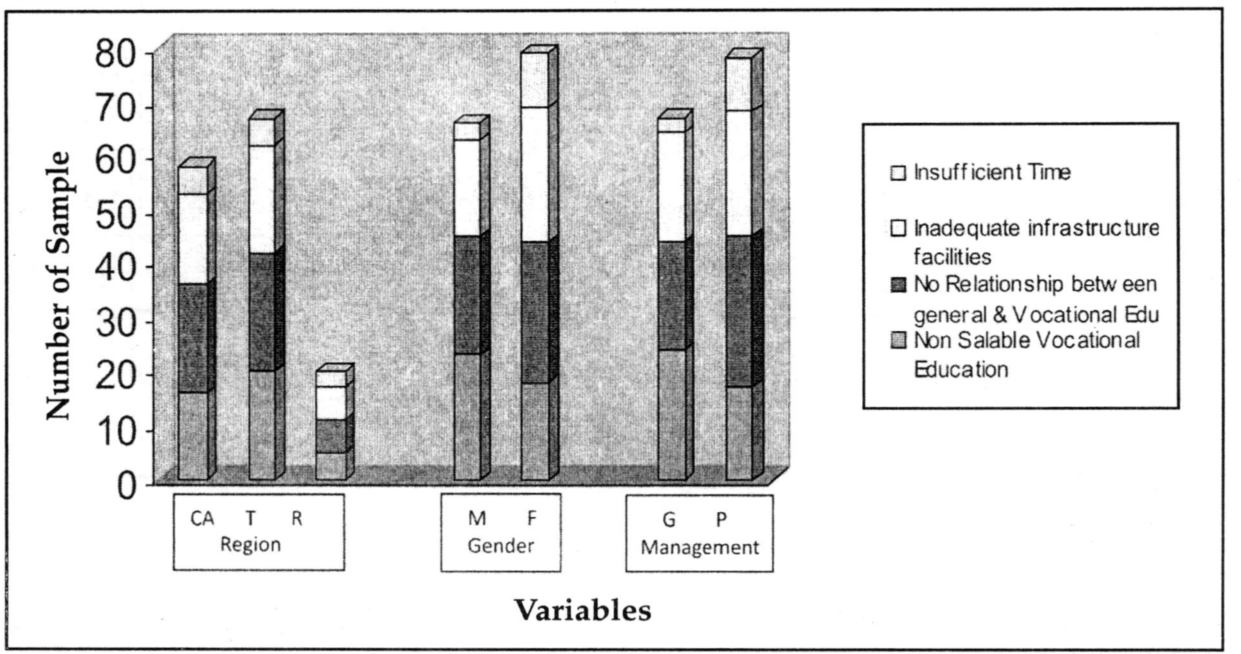

Fig. 5.4: **Problems in Relation to Vocational Education**

responded that the non-saleable of vocational education (G-35.8%, P-21.7%) was sufficient whereas the private management teachers that there was no relationship between general and vocational education (G-29.8%, P-35.8%) and also insufficient time for vocational education courses (G-44%, P-12.8%).

This finding supports the finding of Dhote, A.K. (1991) which correlates with the finding that "non-recognition of vocational courses for employment".

Responses of the Teachers Towards Vocational Education Examination Pattern

To know the responses of the teachers towards vocational education examination pattern, the investigator analysed the collected data with the help the percentage of their responses on the questionnaire and the results obtained are presented in Table 5.39.

Table 5.39: Need for Additional Facilities

Sl. No.	*Additional Facilities*	*Region*			*Gender*		*Management*	
		Coastal Andhra	*Telan-gana*	*Rayala-seema*	*Male*	*Female*	*Govt.*	*Private*
1.	Rooms	17.2% (10)	18% (12)	15% (3)	19.6% (13)	15% (12)	17.9% (12)	16.6% (13)
2.	Raw material	12% (7)	15% (10)	10% (2)	16.6% (11)	10% (8)	12% (8)	14.1% (11)
3.	Machinery	19% (11)	18% (12)	20% (4)	25.7% (17)	12.6% (10)	14.9% (10)	21.8% (17)
4.	Vocational Trained Teaching	20.6% (12)	19% (13)	15% (3)	15.1% (10)	26.5% (21)	17.9% (12)	20.5% (16)
5.	Funds	31% (18)	30% (20)	40% (8)	22.7% (15)	35% (21)	37.3% (25)	26.9% (21)
	Total	**58**	**67**	**20**	**66**	**79**	**67**	**78**

Table 5.39 shows that more number of teachers from all the three regions of Andhra Pradesh i.e. Coastal Andhra, Telangana and Rayalaseema expressed that they needed additional facilities to impart vocational education for the hearing impaired students. Their responses are as follows: Need for additional rooms (CA-17.2%, T-18%, R-15%), Raw material (CA-12%, T-15%, R-10%), Machinery (CA-19%, T-18%, R-20%), Vocational trained teachers (A-20.6%, T-19%, R-15%) and Funds (CA-31%, T-30%, R-40%).

With reference to the gender variable both male and female teachers with a slight difference expressed that they needed additional facilities to impart vocational education to the hearing impaired students in special schools. Their responses are as follows:

(i) Requirement of additional rooms (M-19.6%, F-15%);

(ii) Machinery (M-25.7%, F-12.6%);

(iii) Raw material (M-15.1%, F-26.5%);

(iv) Vocational Trained teachers (M-15.1%, F-26.5%).

Among all the above-mentioned items more than 90% of both male (93.9%) and female teachers (94.9%) indicated that they needed financial assistance or funds.

The management variable shows that the teachers from both government and private managements equally expressed that they needed additional rooms to impart vocational education (G-17.9%, P-16.6%). Whereas when compared to private management schools, more number of government school teachers pointed out the need for Raw material (G-12%, P-14.1%) and machinery (G-14.9%, P-21.8%).

But when compared to teachers working in government schools, more number of teachers working in private management schools expressed that they needed more number of vocational trained teachers (G-17.9%, P-20.5%). Irrespective of management (G-37.3%, P-26.9%) the teachers expressed that they needed financial assistance for vocational education courses.

This finding supports the finding of Reddy (1984) which correlates with the finding that, "inadequate physical, infrastructure facilities, non-availability of funds in imparting vocational education."

Responses of the Teachers Towards Vocational Education Examination Pattern

To know the responses of the teachers towards vocational education examination pattern, the investigator analysed the collected data with the help the percentage of their responses on the questionnaire and the results obtained are presented in Table 5.40.

Table 5.40: Expected Changes through Vocational Education

Sl. No.	*Expected out come*	*Region*			*Gender*		*Management*	
		Coastal Andhra	*Telan-gana*	*Rayala-seema*	*Male*	*Female*	*Govt.*	*Private*
1.	Improvement in the Economic status	22.4% (13)	31.3% (21)	25% (5)	27.2% (18)	26.5% (21)	32.8% (22)	21.7% (17)
2.	Self Dependent/ Economic independent	37.9% (22)	37.3% (25)	40% (8)	36.3% (24)	39.2% (31)	34.3% (23)	41% (32)
3.	Self confidence/ Self Respect	39.6% (23)	31.3% (21)	35% (7)	36.3% (24)	34.1% (27)	32.8% (22)	37.1% (29)
4.	Self-Esteem	43% (25)	46% (31)	50% (10)	51.5% (34)	39.2% (31)	46.2% (31)	45% (35)

Note: The teachers responded more than one outcome.

Table 5.40 reveals that more number of samples from all the three regions of Andhra Pradesh i.e. Coastal Andhra (43%), Telangana (46%) and Rayalaseema (50%) expressed that by providing vocational education to the hearing impaired students their self-esteem would be enhanced. In the same way they also expressed the following:

(i) Self-confidence/self-respect (A-39.6%, T-31.3%, R-35%).

(ii) Self-dependent/Economic independence (A-37.9%, T-37.3%, R.40%).

(iii) Economic status enhancement (A-22.4%, T-31.3%, R-25%).

As far as gender variable was concerned more number of male teachers (51.5%) when compared to female teachers (39.2%) expressed that the self esteem of the deaf students would be enhanced by providing vocational education training and also their self - confidence would be developed (M-36.3%, F-34.1%) whereas when compared to male teachers (36.3%) female teachers (39.2%) indicated that the hearing impaired students would become self dependents. But both male and female samples equally (M-27.2%, F-26.3%) responded that the deaf individuals' economic status would be developed through vocational training.

The management variable shows that the majority of the government school (32.8%) respondents when compared to the (P-21.7%) private schools expressed that through vocational training courses the economic status of the deaf child might be improved whereas the private management respondents compared to government management confused that the self confidence in them would be increased (G-32.8%, P-37.1%) as well as they would become self dependent (G-34.3%, P-41%) whereas both the government (46.2%) and private (45%) management sample equally expressed that the self-esteem of the hearing impaired students would be enhanced through introducing and providing training in vocational education courses.

This finding supports the finding of Mery and Maria (2001) and also, Favidah, Serjul Huq (2003), which correlates, with the finding that "it helps in the enhancement of the self esteem and will help in economic independence and successful living."

Responses of the Teachers Towards Vocational Education Examination Pattern

To know the responses of the teachers towards vocational education examination pattern, the investigator analysed the collected data with the help the percentage of their responses on the questionnaire and the results obtained are presented in Table 5.41.

Table 5.41: Preference of Vocational Education of Hearing Impaired Students

Sl. No.	*Items*	*Region*			*Gender*		*Management*	
		Coastal Andhra	*Telan-gana*	*Rayala-seema*	*Male*	*Female*	*Govt.*	*Private*
1.	Tailoring	26.7% (64)	27.7% (75)	18.9% (17)	25.7% (99)	27.8% (57)	22.6% (61)	29.79% (95)
2.	T.V./Radio Mechanism	19.6% (47)	15.4% (40)	15.6% (14)	17.4% (67)	16.6% (34)	2.2% (6)	29.5% (95)
3.	Computer	33.3% (80)	44% (116)	53.3% (48)	40% (154)	41.8% (90)	44.8% (106)	38.3% (138)
4.	Mechanic	-	1.5% (4)	1.1% (1)	1% (4)	0.5% (1)	1.5% (4)	0.3% (1)
5.	Any other	20.4% (49)	13.5% (35)	11.1% (10)	15.8% (61)	16.1% (33)	26.2% (63)	8.6% (31)
	Total	**240**	**270**	**90**	**385**	**215**	**240**	**360**

Table 5.41 shows that majority of the students in all the regions of Andhra Pradesh preferred Computer Education. The order of preference for vocational education in the Coastal Andhra region was given as computer training (33.3%), tailoring (26.7%), and any other (20.4%). Nobody preferred Mechanical field. The order of preference for vocational education of Telangana region Students was as follows: Computer (44%), Tailoring (28.8%), TV/Radio Machanism (15.4%) and any other (13.5%) Mechanic (1.5%), whereas the order of preference for vocational education given by Rayalaseema Students was computer (53.3%), tailoring (18.9%), TV/Radio Mechanism

(15.6%), any other (11.1%) and Mechanic (1.1%). Among the three regions the most preferred vocational education was Computer education and the least preferred was Mechanic. This may be because of the influence of the Information Technology in all the fields of life. The glamour of both the status and monitory benefit may also be one of the reasons.

The gender variable shows that there was no difference in the first order of preference for vocational education by the students. Both boys and girls preferred Computer education, and the least Mechanic education. The reason may be because of their disability, cultural factors etc. The order of preference for vocational education was given by the male students: Computer education (40%), Tailoring (25.7%), TV/Radio Mechanism (17.4%), Any other (15.8%) and Mechanism (1%). Whereas the female students showed the order of preference as: Computer (41.8%), Tailoring (27.8%), TV/Radio Mechanism (16.6%), any other (16.1%) and Mechanic (0.5%).

When considered the management variable there was no difference in the most preferred and least preferred vocational education areas. Among the government school students the order of preference for vocational education was observed as follows:

(i) Computer education (44%)

(ii) Any other (26.2%)

(iii) Tailoring (22.6%)

(iv) TV/Radio Mechanism (2.2%)

(v) Mechanic (1.5%).

The Private school students gave the order of preference for vocational education was as follows:

(i) Computer education (38.3%)

(ii) Tailoring (29.7%)

(iii) TV/Radio Mechanism (29.5%)

(iv) Any other (8.6%)

(v) Mechanic (0.3%).

This finding supports the finding of Muthaiah (1989) which correlates with the finding that "Vocational Education courses imparted are not in accordance with the interests and aspirations of the children.

Responses of the Teachers Towards Vocational Education Examination Pattern

To know the responses of the teachers towards vocational education examination pattern, the investigator analysed the collected data with the help the percentage of their responses on the questionnaire and the results obtained are presented in Table 5.42.

Table 5.42: Undergoing Vocational Education Training

Sl. No.	*Items*	*Region*			*Gender*		*Management*	
		Coastal Andhra	*Telan-gana*	*Rayala-seema*	*Male*	*Female*	*Govt.*	*Private*
1.	Tailoring	46.6% (112)	29.6% (80)	42.2% (38)	31.1% (120)	51.1% (110)	25% (60)	47.2% (170)
2.	Book-Binding	15.8% (38)	13.7% (37)	55.5% (50)	25.9% (100)	11.6% (25)	15.8% (38)	24.2% (87)
3.	Type-Writing	-	2.6% (7)	-	2.5% (7)	-	-	1.9% (7)
4.	Candle making	5% (12)	0.8% (2)	2.2% (2)	2.5% (10)	2.7% (6)	1.6% (4)	3.3% (12)
5.	Carpentry	9.5% (23)	6.6% (18)	-	10.6% (41)	-	11.6% (28)	8.6% (13)
6.	Computer	8.3% (20)	3.7% (10)	-	5.4% (21)	4.1% (9)	4.1% (10)	5.5% (20)
7.	TV/Radio Mechanism	12.5 (30)	11.1% (30)	-	10.6% (41)	7.6% (19)	16.6% (40)	5.5% (20)
8.	Any other	2% (5)	(86)	-	11.6% (45)	21.3% (46)	25% (60)	8.6% (31)
	Total	**240**	**270**	**90**	**385**	**215**	**240**	**360**

From Table 5.42 it is evident that the hearing impaired students of three regions of Andhra Pradesh expressed that they were undergoing vocational training in Tailoring (CA-46.6%, T-29.6%, R-42.2%), Bookbinding (CA-15.8%, T-13.7%, R-55.5%), Typewriting. Only Telangana (2.6%) students were undergoing training in Candle/Basket making (CA-5%, T-0.8%, R-2.2%), Carpentry (CA-9.5%, T-6.6%) and nobody was from Rayalaseema. In Radio/TV mechanism only ane was found from Coastal Andhra (2%) but no one was from Telangana and Rayalaseema. Only Telangana (31.8%) students were getting training any other activity but no one was from Andhra and Rayalaseema regions.

The gender variable points out that both the sexes responded that they are undergoing vocational education training in Tailoring (M-31.1%, F-51.1%), Book binding (M-25.9%, F-11.6%), Typewriting (M-2.5%), Candle/Basket Making (M-2.5%, F-2.7%), Carpentry (M-10.6%), Computer (M-5.4%, M-4.1), Radio/ T.V. mechanism (M-10.6%, F-7.6%) and any other (M-12.9%, F-21.3%).

The management variable shows both the government and private management school were imparting vocational education. When compared to the students of government management schools, more number of private management school students were receiving more variety of vocational education courses as in Tailoring (G-25%, P-47.2%), Book-binding (G-15.8%, P-24.2%), Typewriting (G-0%, P-1.9%), Candle/Basket making (G-1.6%, P.3.3%), Carpentry (G-11.6%, P-8.6%), Computer (G-4.1%, P.5.5%), Radio/TV mechanism (G-16.6%, P-1.3%) and any other (G-25%, P-8.6%).

This finding supports the finding of Chandramani and Kalavani which correlated with the finding that "Vocational Education courses imparted in special school have Tailoring, Bookbinding, Carpentry, Typewriting, Computer, Candle/Basket making and Radio/TV mechanism".

Responses of the Teachers Towards Vocational Education Examination Pattern

To know the responses of the teachers towards vocational education examination pattern, the investigator analysed the collected data with the help the percentage of their responses on the questionnaire and the results obtained are presented in Table 5.43.

Table 5.43: Onset of Vocational Education

Sl. No.	Period	Region			Gender		Management	
		Coastal Andhra	Telan-gana	Rayala-seema	Male	Female	Govt.	Private
1.	6th	12.5% (30)	11.1% (30)	38.8% (35)	14.2% (55)	18.6% (40)	14.5% (35)	16.6% (60)
2.	7th	8.3% (20)	7.4% (20)	15.5% (14)	9.5% (36)	8.3% (18)	4.5% (11)	11.9% (43)
3.	8th	52% (125)	44.4% (120)	45.6% (41)	45.6% (172)	53% (114)	40.8% (98)	52.2% (188)
4.	9th	2% (5)	3.7% (10)	-	2.5% (10)	2.3% (5)	2.5% (6)	2.5% (8)
6.	No training	25% (60)	33.3% (90)	-	29% (112)	17.6% (38)	37.5% (90)	16.6% (60)
	Total	**240**	**270**	**90**	**385**	**215**	**240**	**360**

The data in Table 5.43 shows that from the three regions of Andhra Pradesh, more number of Coastal Andhra (52%), Telangana (44.4%) and Rayalaseema (45.5%) students expressed that they were getting vocational education from class 8th onwards. A least number of students of the Coastal Andhra (2%) and Telangana (3.7%) responded that had vocational education from 9th class. Whereas the least number of Rayalaseema students (15.5%) expressed that they had started vocational education from 7th class. But the Coastal Andhra (25%) and Telangana (33.3%) students responded that they did not have vocational education training in any class. With reference to the gender variable, both boys (45%) and girls (53%) responded equally that they had started vocational education training from 8th class. Very few respondents of both the sexes (B-2.5%, G-2.3%) expressed that they had started vocational education training from 9th class. Whereas boys (29%) and girls (17.6%) expressed that they did not have any vocational education training from any class.

The management variable indicates that more number of private school students (52.2%) compared to the government school students (40.8%) expressed that they had started learning vocational training from 8th class. Whereas very few private management school students (16.6%) expressed that they had no vocational education. Whereas government management school students (37.5%) expressed that they were not undergoing any vocational education training.

Responses of the Teachers Towards Vocational Education Examination Pattern

To know the responses of the teachers towards vocational education examination pattern, the investigator analysed the collected data with the help the percentage of their responses on the questionnaire and the results obtained are presented in Table 5.44.

Table 5.44: Vocational training from various stages

Sl. No.	*Stage*	*Region*			*Gender*		*Management*	
		Coastal Andhra	*Telan-gana*	*Rayala-seema*	*Boys*	*Girls*	*Govt.*	*Private*
1.	Primary	18.8% (45)	7.7% (21)	11% (10)	11.9% (46)	13.9% (30)	10.4% (25)	14.2% (51)
2.	Upper Primary	41.3% (99)	51.8% (140)	50% (45)	38.9% (150)	62.3% (134)	54.1% (130)	42.7% (154)
3.	Secondary	40% (96)	40.3% (109)	38.8% (35)	49% (189)	23.7% (51)	35.4% (85)	43% (155)
	Total	**240**	**270**	**90**	**385**	**215**	**240**	**360**

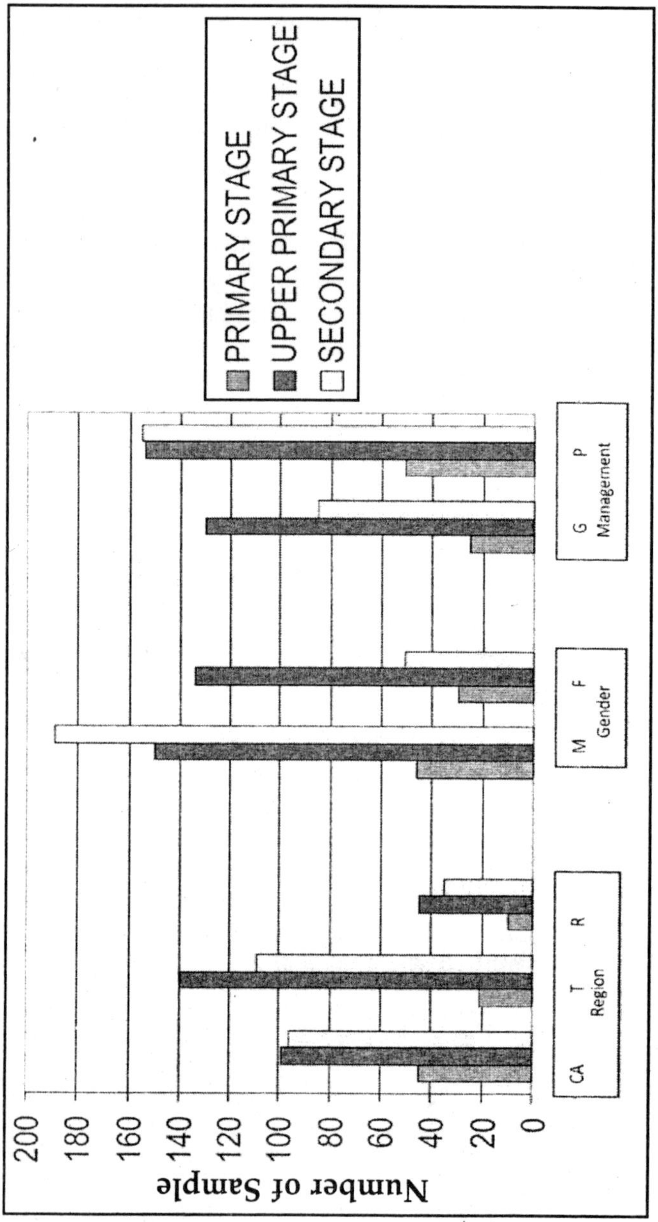

Fig. 5.5: **Vocational Training from Various States**

Table 5.44 shows that majority of the hearing impaired students from the three regions of Coastal Andhra, Telangana and Rayalaseema (CA-41.3%, T-51.8%, R-50%) expressed that they needed vocational training from the upper primary level. The least number of students (CA-18.8%, T-7.7%, R.11%) preferred it from the primary level.

Considering the gender variable, the majority of the boys (49%) preferred that they needed vocational training from the secondary level, whereas girls (62.3%) preferred it from the upper primary level. The least number of both the boys and girls (M-11.9%, F-13.9%) preferred it from the upper primary level.

With reference to the management variables the students who were studying in government schools (F-54.1%) expressed that the vocation training should be from the upper primary level. Very few students (10.4%) expressed it should be from the primary level. When compared to the government management school students from private management school, they equally preferred that it should be from the upper primary level (42.7%) and the secondary level (43%). Whereas very few expressed (14.2%) that it should be from the primary level.

Responses of the Teachers Towards Vocational Education Examination Pattern

To know the responses of the teachers towards vocational education examination pattern, the investigator analysed the collected data with the help the percentage of their responses on the questionnaire and the results obtained are presented in Table 5.45.

The data in Table 5.45 shows that among the three regions of Andhra Pradesh, all the students (100%) from Rayalaseema expressed that they had no fixed duration of time to learn the vocational courses. Majority of the Coastal Andhra (80.4%) and Telangana (87%) students expressed the same view. Both the Coastal Andhra and Telangana students (CA-5.4%, T-7%) said that they had only one-year duration for vocational education courses. The Coastal Andhra and Telangana students (CA-13.5%, T-4.4%)

conferred that they had 2-year duration for vocational education, whereas the least number of students (CA-0.8%, T-1.5%) revealed that they had 3 years duration for vocational education. None from the Rayalaseema expressed any view.

Table 5.45: Duration of Vocational Education Courses

Sl. No.	Time Duration	Region			Gender		Management	
		Coastal Andhra	*Telan-gana*	*Rayala-seema*	*Male*	*Female*	*Govt.*	*Private*
1.	1 Year	5.4% (13)	7% (19)	-	6% (23)	4.2% (9)	7.9% (19)	3.6% (13)
2.	2 Years	13.3% (32)	44% (12)	-	4.4% (17)	12.6% (27)	10.4% (15)	5.3% (19)
3.	3 Years	0.8% (2)	1.5% (4)	-	1.6% (6)	-	2.5% (6)	-
4.	No Time Limit	80.4% (193)	87% (235)	100% (90)	88.1% (339)	83.3% (179)	79.2% (190)	90.1% (328)
	Total	**240**	**270**	**90**	**385**	**215**	**240**	**360**

With reference to the gender variable, both the male and female students equally (M-88.1%, F-83.3%) expressed that there was no time limit to learn the vocational education courses. Very few (1.6%) male students spelt that there was three years of time duration whereas there was no response from the female students. Only 6% of boys and 4.2% of girls students responded for 1-year duration and 4.4% of boys and 12.6% of girls students for two years of duration. It may be due to lack of knowledge with regard to course duration.

With regard to the management variable most of the students from both the government and private schools (G-79.2% P-91.1%) responded that there was no one to learn vocational courses. Very few government school students (2.5%) expressed that, there was 3 years duration to learn vocational courses, none from the private school student responded for 3 year course duration.

This finding supports the finding of Patel (1991) finding which correlates with "the duration of time or time allotted to vocational education courses is too inadequate; to teach and practice it."

Responses of the Teachers Towards Vocational Education Examination Pattern

To know the responses of the teachers towards vocational education examination pattern, the investigator analysed the collected data with the help the percentage of their responses on the questionnaire and the results obtained are presented in Table 5.46.

Table 5.46: Method of Teaching of Vocational Courses

Sl. No.	*Method of Teaching*	*Region*			*Gender*		*Management*	
		Coastal Andhra	*Telan-gana*	*Rayala-seema*	*Male*	*Female*	*Govt.*	*Private*
1.	Lecture Method	16.6% (40)	14.4% (39)	22.2% (20)	15.5% (60)	18.1% (39)	16.6% (40)	16.3% (59)
2.	Activity Method	12.9% (31)	11.8% (32)	20% (18)	12.7% (49)	14.8% (32)	11.2% (27)	15% (54)
3.	More Lecture and Less Activity	62.5% (150)	31.8% (86)	35.5% (32)	43.8% (169)	46% (99)	52% (125)	39.7% (143)
4.	More Activity and Less Lecture	1.2% (3)	27.7% (75)	3.7% (10)	17.9% (69)	8.8% (19)	14.8% (40)	13.3% (48)
5.	Both are equal	6.6% (16)	14% (38)	3.7% (10)	9.8% (38)	12.1% (26)	3.3% (8)	15.5% (56)
	Total	**240**	**270**	**90**	**385**	**215**	**240**	**360**

Table 5.46 shows that the majority of the hearing impaired students from Coastal Andhra region (62.5%) expressed that the method of teaching vocational courses was lecture method rather than activity method. The hearing impaired students from both the Rayalaseema (35.5%) and Telangana (31.8%) responded in same manner. Very few hearing impaired students from the

Coastal Andhra (1.2%) and Rayalaseema (3.7%) expressed that there was more activity and less lecture method. Among these regions the hearing-impaired students from the Telangana (27.7%) confused that there was more activity and less lecture method in teaching vocational education courses.

With reference to gender variable, the majority of the boys (43.8%) and girls (46%) responded that the teachers were using more lecture method and giving less importance to activity. Very few students expressed that (M-9.8%, F-12.1%) the teachers were using both the lecture and activity method equally.

When considering management variable, the hearing impaired students from both the government and private schools (G-52%, P-39.7%) expressed that their teachers were using more lecture method rather than activity method to teach vocational Education courses. There was no much difference in government and private management schools in the method of teaching vocational education courses. Few students of government schools (3.3%) responded that their teachers were using both lecture and activity method equally. Whereas the least number of private school students (13.3%) responded that their teachers were using activity method more than the lecture method.

From the above it may be drawn that the majority of the students from all the three regions, boys and girls and from government and private management schools stated that the method of instruction in vocational training was more lecture oriented and less activity oriented.

This finding supports the finding of Joshi (1992) and Patel (1991) which correlates that "there is lack of practical training due to lack of tools, equipment and material."

Responses of the Teachers Towards Vocational Education Examination Pattern

To know the responses of the teachers towards vocational education examination pattern, the investigator analysed the collected data with the help the percentage of their responses on the questionnaire and the results obtained are presented in Table 5.47.

Table 5.47: Source of Raw Material

Sl. No.	*Source of Raw Material*	*Region*			*Gender*		*Management*	
		Coastal Andhra	*Telan-gana*	*Rayala-seema*	*Male*	*Female*	*Govt.*	*Private*
1.	School	37.7% (91)	41.9% (109)	33.3% (30)	36% (139)	42.8% (91)	24.8% (67)	71.6% (229)
2.	By their own	22.1% (53)	7.7% (21)	-	14.5% (56)	8.8% (18)	12.6% (34)	11% (40)
3.	No Raw material	40% (96)	54% (140)	66.7% (60)	49.4% (190)	51.7% (106)	57.9% (139)	25.2% (91)
	Total	**240**	**270**	**90**	**385**	**215**	**240**	**360**

From the Table 5.47 it is evident that more number of sample from all the three regions of Andhra Pradesh i.e. Coastal Andhra (40%), Telangana (54%) and Rayalaseema (66.7%) expressed that there was lack of raw material to learn the vocational education courses. The least number of students from the Coastal Andhra (22.1%) and Telangana (7.7%) have responded that they were using their own raw material.

With reference to the gender variable, both the boys (49.4%) and girls (51.7%) students responded that there was no supply of raw material to teach the vocational courses. Few boys (14.5%) and girls (8.8%) expressed that they were using their own material to learn the course.

With reference to the management variable, when compared to private schools (25.2%) majority of the government school students (57.9%) expressed that they were not using any raw material. In contrast, majority of the private school srudents (71.6%) expressed that they were using raw material which was provided by the school management.

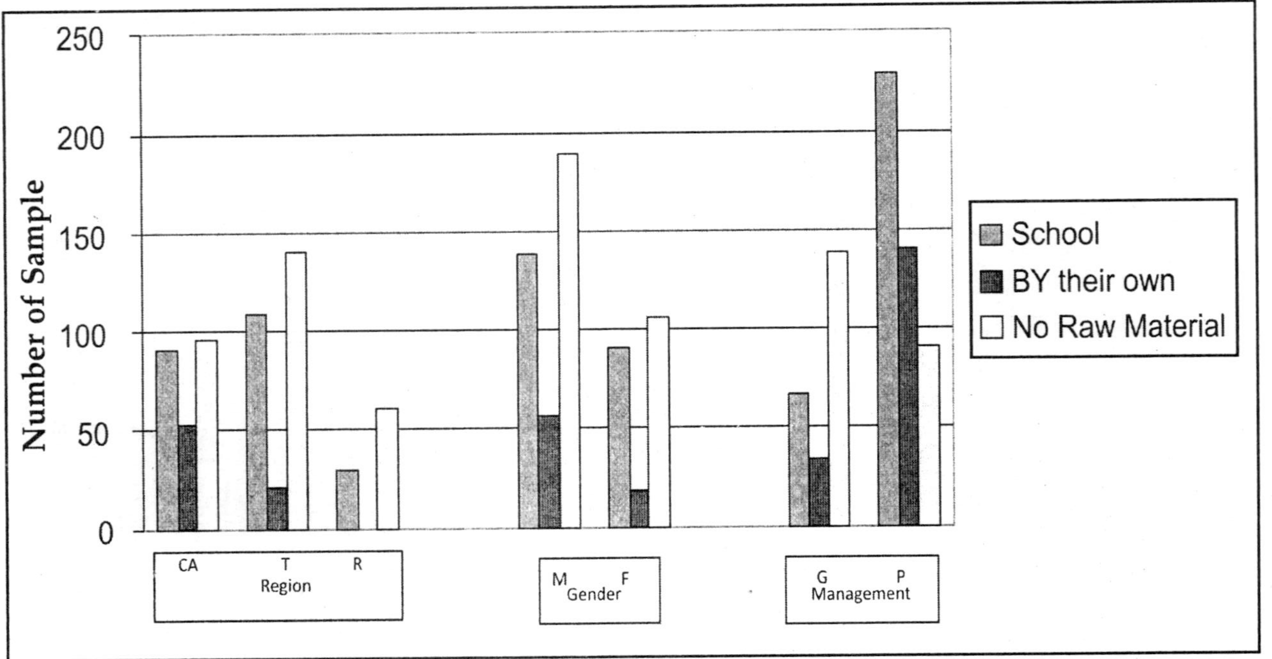

Fig. 5.6: **Source of Raw Material**

This finding supports the finding of Misra and Varma (1990) which correlates with the finding that "no provision is made for raw materials and other contingencies".

Responses of the Teachers Towards Vocational Education Examination Pattern

To know the responses of the teachers towards vocational education examination pattern, the investigator analysed the collected data with the help of chi-square test and the results obtained are presented in Table 5.48.

Hypothesis

There is no significant difference in the region wise expressed responses of the hearing impaired students on the "availability of sufficient rooms for vocational education courses".

Table 5.48: Responses of the hearing impaired students on the "availability of sufficient rooms for vocational education courses"

Regions in A.P.	*Yes*	*No*	*Total*	χ^2
Coastal Andhra	30	210	240	
Telangana	110	160	270	51.208*
Rayalaseema	30	60	90	
Total	**170**	**430**	**600**	

* Significant.

From Table 5.48 it is observed that the calculated Chi-square value of the region wise responses of the Hearing Impaired students is 51.208 which is greater than the table value of 6.64 and is significant at 0.01 level. Therefore, it can be stated that region of the students has significant value on their responses with regard to the availability of rooms for vocational education courses in their schools. Hence, it can be said that the formulated hypothesis is rejected.

From the above table it is clear that most of the students (430 out of 600) categorically stated that the rooms for vocational educational courses were not sufficient whereas only 170 students responded positively. Among the three regions most of the Coastal Andhra students (210 out of 240) compared to the Telangana and Rayalaseema opined that the rooms available for vocational courses were sufficient.

Responses of the Teachers Towards Vocational Education Examination Pattern

To know the responses of the teachers towards vocational education examination pattern, the investigator analysed the collected data with the help of chi-square test and the results obtained are presented in Table 5.49.

Hypothesis

There is no significant difference in the gender wise expressed responses of the hearing impaired students with regard to the "availability of rooms for vocational education courses".

Table 5.49: Responses of the hearing impaired students on the "availability of rooms for vocational education"

Gender	*Yes*	*No*	*Total*	χ^2
Boys	225	160	385	2.00**
Girls	112	103	215	
Total	**337**	**263**	**600**	

** Not significant.

It is clear from Table 5.49 that the calculated Chi-square value of the gender wise responses of the students is 2.00 which is less than the table value of 6.64 and not significant at 0.01 level. Therefore it can be stated that the gender of the students has not any significant value on their responses with regard to the availability of rooms for vocational education. Hence the formulated hypothesis is retained.

It is evident from the above table that most of the boys (225 out of 385) and girls (112 out of 215) stated that the rooms available for vocational courses were adequate.

Responses of the Teachers Towards Vocational Education Examination Pattern

To know the responses of the teachers towards vocational education examination pattern, the investigator analysed the collected data with the help of chi-square test and the results obtained are presented in Table 5.50.

Hypothesis

There is no significant difference in the responses of the hearing impaired students in relation to the type of management of the school in which they are studying with regard to "availability rooms for vocational education Courses".

Table 5.50: Responses of the hearing impaired students on the "availability of rooms for vocational education courses"

Management	*Yes*	*No*	*Total*	χ^2
Government	40	200	240	
Private	130	230	360	25.86*
Total	**170**	**430**	**600**	

* Significant.

The data in Table 5.50 shows that the calculated Chi-square value of the responses of the hearing impaired students in relation to management of the school is 25.86 which is greater than the table value of 6.64 and is significant at 0.01 level. Therefore, it is assumed that the hearing impaired students in different management schools have significant value on their responses with regard to the "availability of rooms for vocational education". Hence, it can be stated that the formulated hypothesis is rejected.

From the above table it is evident that the majority of the students (200 out of 240) from government schools stated that the availability of rooms for vocational training were not sufficient, whereas the students from private schools (230 out of 360) spoke positively.

Responses of the Teachers Towards Vocational Education Examination Pattern

To know the responses of the teachers towards vocational education examination pattern, the investigator analysed the collected data with the help of chi-square test and the results obtained are presented in Table 5.51.

Hypothesis

There is no significant difference in the region wise responses of the hearing impaired students with regard to the "adequate machinery for vocational education courses".

Table 5.51: Region wise responses of the hearing impaired students on the "adequate machinery for vocational education"

Regions in A.P.	*Yes*	*No*	*Total*	χ^2
Coastal Andhra	149	91	240	
Telangana	138	132	270	6.229*
Rayalaseema	50	40	90	
Total	**337**	**263**	**600**	

* Significant.

From Table 5.51 it is observed that the calculated Chi-square value of the region wise responses of the hearing impaired students is 6.229, which is greater than the table value of 5.99% and is significant at 0.05 level. Therefore, it is assumed that the region of the students has significant value on their responses with regard to the machinery for vocational education courses are adequate. Hence, it can be said that the formulated hypothesis is rejected.

It is evident that the majority of the teachers (337 out of 600) from all the three regions opined that the machinery for vocational education courses was adequate. Whereas some teachers (263 out of 600) stated that it was inadequate. Most of the teachers of Telangana (132 out of 270) compared to the Coastal Andhra and Rayalaseema responded negatively.

Responses of the Teachers Towards Vocational Education Examination Pattern

To know the responses of the teachers towards vocational education examination pattern, the investigator analysed the collected data with the help of chi-square test and the results obtained are presented in Table 5.52.

Hypothesis

There is no significant difference in the gender wise responses of the hearing impaired students with regard to the "availability of machinery for vocational education courses".

Table 5.52: Gender wise responses of the hearing impaired students on the "availability of machinery for vocational education courses"

Gender	*Yes*	*No*	*Total*	χ^2
Boys	90	295	385	
Girls	55	160	215	0.225**
Total	**145**	**455**	**600**	

** Not significant.

It is noticed from Table 5.52 that the calculated Chi-square value of the responses of the gender wise hearing impaired students is 0.225 which is less than the table value of 6.64 and is not significant at 0.01 level. Therefore, it is assumed that the gender of the students does not have any significant value on their responses with regard to the machinery for vocational education courses are adequate. Hence, it can be said that the formulated hypothesis is retained.

From the above table it is evident that the majority of the boys (295 out of 385) and girls (160 out of 215) opined that the available machinery for vocational courses was inadequate.

Responses of the Teachers Towards Vocational Education Examination Pattern

To know the responses of the teachers towards vocational education examination pattern, the investigator analysed the collected data with the help of chi-square test and the results obtained are presented in Table 5.53.

Hypothesis

There is no significant difference in the responses of the hearing impaired students in relation to type of management of school in which they are studying with regard to the "adequate machinery for vocational education courses".

Table 5.53: Responses of the hearing impaired students in relation to type of management of school with respect to "Adequate machinery for vocational education courses"

Management	*Yes*	*No*	*Total*	χ^2
Government	10	230	240	
Private	21	339	360	0.511**
Total	**31**	**569**	**600**	

** Not significant.

It is observed from Table 5.53 that the calculated Chi-square value of the responses of the Hearing Impaired students in relation to type of management of schools is 0.511 which is less than the table value of 3.84 and is not significant at 0.01 level. Therefore, it can be stated that the type of management of the school in which the students are studying has significant value on their responses with regard to the availability of machinery for vocational education. Hence, it is stated that the formulated hypothesis is retained.

From the above table it is evident that the majority of the students studying in government (230 out of 240) and private (339 out of 360) schools stated that the available machinery for vocational education courses was not adequate.

Responses of the Teachers Towards Vocational Education Examination Pattern

To know the responses of the teachers towards vocational education examination pattern, the investigator analysed the collected data with the help of chi-square test and the results obtained are presented in Table 5.54.

Hypothesis

There is no significant difference in the gender wise responses of the hearing impaired students with regard to the "availability of adequate number of computers".

Table 5.54: Genderwise responses of the Hearing Impaired students on the "availability of adequate number of computers"

Regions in A.P.	*Yes*	*No*	*Total*	χ^2
Coastal Andhra	30	210	240	
Telangana	110	160	270	51.208*
Rayalaseema	30	60	90	
Total	**170**	**430**	**600**	

* Significant.

Table 5.54 reveals that the calculated Chi-square value of the responses of the region wise Hearing Impaired students is 51.208 which is greater than 9.21 and is significant at 0.01 level. Therefore, it is assumed that the responses of the students of the three regions have significant impact on their responses with regard to the availability of computers for vocational training. Hence, it can be said that the formulated hypothesis is rejected.

It is therefore evident that the majority of the teachers from the Coastal Andhra (210 out of 240) and Rayalaseema

(60 out of 90) opined that the availability of computers for learning computer education was not sufficient. Whereas teachers from the Telangana (110 out of 270) when compared to the Coastal Andhra and Rayalaseema stated that the availability of computers was adequate.

Responses of the Teachers Towards Vocational Education Examination Pattern

To know the responses of the teachers towards vocational education examination pattern, the investigator analysed the collected data with the help of chi-square test and the results obtained are presented in Table 5.55.

Hypothesis

There is no significant difference in the gender wise responses of the hearing impaired students with respect to the "availability of adequate number of computer for vocational training".

Table 5.55: Responses of the Hearing Impaired students on the availability of Computers for vocational training

Gender	*Yes*	*No*	*Total*	χ^2
Boys	110	275	385	
Girls	60	155	215	0.0051**
Total	**170**	**430**	**600**	

** Not significant.

It is observed from Table 5.55 that the responses of the hearing impaired students are distributed and Chi-square valued was calculated. The obtained Chi-square value is 0.0051 which is less than the table value of 6.64 and not significant at 0.01 level. Therefore, it is opined that the gender wise responses of the students region wise do not have any significant impact on the "availability of adequate number of Computers". Hence, it is said that the formulated hypothesis is accepted.

As per the above table the majority of the boys (275 out of 385) and girls (155 out of 215) responded that the available Computers for training computer operations were not sufficient.

Responses of the Teachers Towards Vocational Education Examination Pattern

To know the responses of the teachers towards vocational education examination pattern, the investigator analysed the collected data with the help of chi-square test and the results obtained are presented in Table 5.56.

Hypothesis

There is no significant difference in the responses of the hearing impaired students in relation to the type of management of the school in which they are studying with regard to "availability of computers for vocational courses".

Table 5.56: Responses of the hearing impaired students in relation to type of management of the school on the "availability of Computers for vocational training"

Management	*Yes*	*No*	*Total*	χ^2
Government	10	230	240	
Private	21	339	360	0.511**
Total	**31**	**569**	**600**	

** Not significant.

It is apparent from the Table 5.56 that the calculated Chi-square value of the responses of the Hearing Impaired students in relation to management of the school is 0.511 which is less than the table value of 9.21 and not significant at 0.01 level. Therefore, it is assumed that the responses of the hearing impaired students of different management schools have significant value on their responses with regard to "availability of Computers for vocational training". Hence, it can be stated that the formulated hypothesis is retained.

From the above table the students studying in government as well private management schools (569 out of 600) responded that the available Computers for learning computer operations were not sufficient.

Responses of the Teachers Towards Vocational Education Examination Pattern

To know the responses of the teachers towards vocational education examination pattern, the investigator analysed the collected data with the help the percentage of their responses on the questionnaire and the results obtained are presented in Table 5.57.

Table 5.57: Type of Vocational Education Examination

Sl. No.	Type of Examination	Region			Gender		Management	
		Coastal Andhra	Telan-gana	Rayala-seema	Male	Female	Govt.	Private
1.	Theory based	-	-	14.4% (13)	2.0% (8)	2.3% (5)	-	3.6% (13)
2.	Practical based	2.1% (5)	-	5.5% (5)	1.2% (5)	2.3% (5)	-	2.2% (10)
3.	Theory & Practical	22.9% (55)	6.2% (17)	24.4% (22)	13.2% (51)	20% (43)	7.1% (17)	21.3% (77)
4.	No Examination	75% (180)	93.7% (253)	55.5% (50)	83.4% (321)	75.3% (162)	92.9% (223)	72.2% (260)
	Total	**240**	**270**	**90**	**385**	**215**	**240**	**360**

Table 5.57 states that, the majority of the student sample from all the regions of Andhra Pradesh expressed that they had no vocational education examination (A-75%, T-93.7%, R-55.5%) whereas the least number of samples from the Coastal Andhra (22.9%), Telangana (6.2%) and Rayalaseema (24.4%) responded that they had both theory and practical examination.

With reference to gender variable, both boys and girls (B-85.2%, G-83.9%) expressed that they had no vocational education examination. Whereas the least number of both boys and girls (B-1.2%, G-2.3%) expressed they had practical based examination.

Considering the management variable, both the government school samples (92.2%) and private school students (72.2%) expressed that they had no vocational education examination. Very few private school students (2.2%) expressed that they had only practical based examination.

This finding supports the finding of Mohanty (1986) which correlates with the finding that "lack of practical experience made the students technically unfit for the Job even though they successfully complete their education."

Responses of the Teachers Towards Vocational Education Examination Pattern

To know the responses of the teachers towards vocational education examination pattern, the investigator analysed the collected data with the help the percentage of their responses on the questionnaire and the results obtained are presented in Table 5.58.

Table 5.58: Issue of Certificates for Vocational Education Course

Sl. No.	*Issue of Certificates*	*Region*			*Gender*		*Management*	
		Coastal Andhra	*Telan-gana*	*Rayala-seema*	*Male*	*Female*	*Govt.*	*Private*
1.	Yes	4.1% (10)	5.9% (16)	-	4.6% (18)	3.7% (8)	2% (5)	5.8% (21)
2.	No	95.8% (230)	94% (254)	100% (90)	95.3% (367)	96.2% (207)	97.9% (235)	94.1% (339)
	Total	**240**	**270**	**90**	**385**	**215**	**240**	**350**

From Table 5.58 it is evident that the majority of the students from the three regions of Andhra Pradesh i.e. Coastal Andhra, Rayalaseema and Telangana (CA-95.8%, T-94%, R-100%) expressed that certificates of vocational education courses were not being issued.

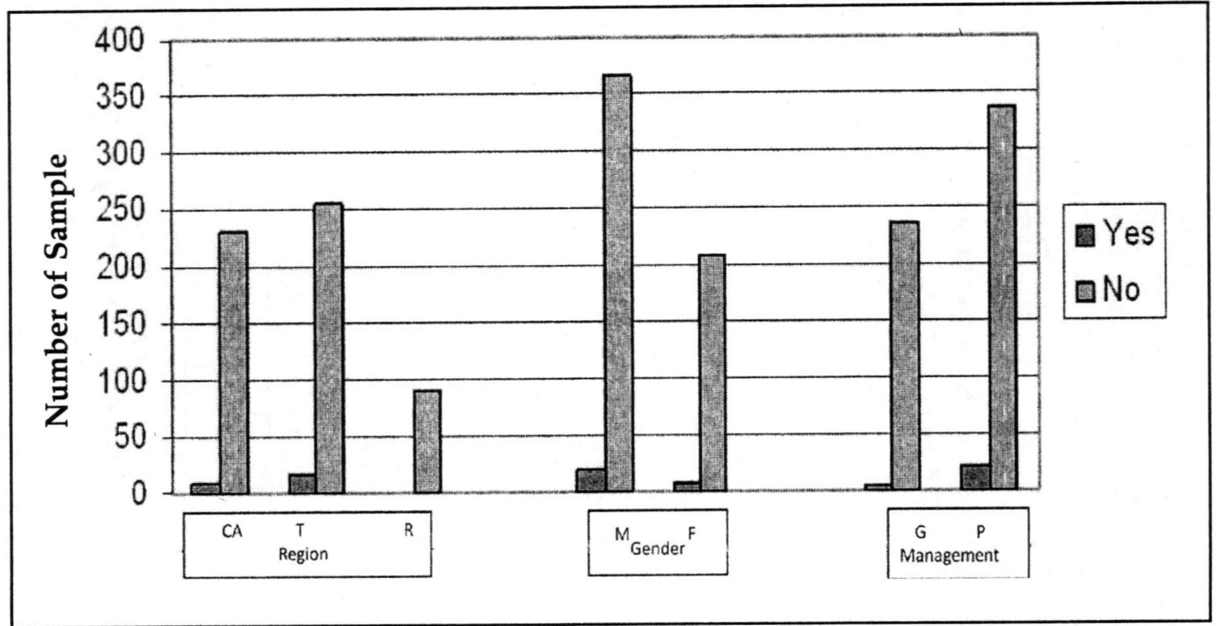

Fig. 5.7: **Issue of Certificate for Vocational Education Course**

With reference to the gender variable both the boys and girls (B-95.3%, G-96.2%) expressed that there were no certificates for vocational education courses.

The management variable reveals that the government (97.9%) and private management school students (94.1%) expressed that there were no certificates for vocational education course.

This finding supports the finding of Dhote (1991) which correlated with the finding that non-recognition of vocational courses for employment.

Responses to the Teachers Towards Vocational Education Examination Pattern

To know the responses of the teachers towards vocational education examination pattern, the investigator analysed the collected data with the help of chi-square test and the results obtained are presented in Table 5.59.

Hypothesis

There is no significant difference in the region wise expressed responses of the students on "opting self employment after completion of vocational education".

Table 5.59: Regionwise responses of the hearing impaired students on "opting self employment after completion of vocational education"

Regions in A.P.	*Yes*	*No*	*Total*	χ^2
Coastal Andhra	149	91	240	
Telangana	138	132	270	6.229*
Rayalaseema	50	40	90	
Total	**337**	**263**	**600**	

* Significant.

From Table 5.59, it is observed that the calculated Chi-square value of the region wise responses of the hearing impaired students is 6.229 which is greater than the table value of 5.99 and is significant at 0.05 level. Therefore, it is assumed that the region of the students has significant value on their responses with regard to opting self employment after completion of vocational course. Hence, it can be said that the formulated hypothesis is rejected.

The data reveal that the majority of the students from all the three regions (337 out of 600) stated that they were in favour of self-employment whereas 263 students out of 600 did not favour.

Responses of the Teachers Towards Vocational Education Examination Pattern

To know the responses of the teachers towards vocational education examination pattern, the investigator analysed the collected data with the help of chi-square test and the results obtained are presented in Table 5.60.

Hypothesis

There is no significant difference in the gender wise responses of the hearing impaired students with regard to the "availability of rooms for vocational education courses".

Table 5.60: Responses of the hearing impaired students on the availability of rooms for vocational education

Gender	*Yes*	*No*	*Total*	χ^2
Boys	225	160	385	
Girls	112	103	215	2.00**
Total	**337**	**263**	**600**	

** Not significant.

It is obvious from Table 5.60 that the calculated Chi-square value of the gender wise responses of the students is 2.00 which is less than the table value of 6.64 and is significant at 0.01 level. Therefore, it can be stated that the gender of the students does not have any significant value on their responses with regard to the "opting of self employment after completion of vocational education". Hence, it is said that the formulated hypothesis is retained.

When compared to girls (112 out of 215) more number of boys (225 out of 385) were in favour of self-employment.

Responses of the Teachers Towards Vocational Education Examination Pattern

To know the responses of the teachers towards vocational education examination pattern, the investigator analysed the collected data with the help of chi-square test and the results obtained are presented in Table 5.61.

Hypothesis

There is no significant difference in the gender wise responses of the hearing impaired students in relation to type of management of the school in which they are studying with regard to the "self-employment after completing the vocational training".

Table 5.61: Responses of the hearing impaired students on "self-employment"

Management	*Yes*	*No*	*Total*	χ^2
Government	70	170	240	
Private	267	93	360	116.62*
Total	**337**	**263**	**600**	

* Significant.

The above table reveals that the calculated Chi-square value of the responses of the students in relation to type of management in which they are studying is 116.62 is grater than the table value of 6.64 and significant at 0.01 level. Therefore, it is assumed that the type of management of the school of the students has significant impact on their responses in "opting self employment after completion of vocational education." Hence, it is stated that the formulated hypothesis is rejected.

From the above table it is obvious that the majority of the students studying government schools (170 out of 240) stated that they were not in favour of self-employment. Whereas the students studying in private management schools (267 out of 360) have responded that they were in favour of self-employment.

Responses of the Teachers Towards Vocational Education Examination Pattern

To know the responses of the teachers towards vocational education examination pattern, the investigator analysed the collected data with the help of chi-square test and the results obtained are presented in Table 5.62.

Hypothesis

There is no significant difference in the region wise responses of the hearing impaired students with regard to the "economic utility of the vocational education courses".

Table 5.62: Responses of the hearing impaired students on the "economic utility of the vocational courses"

Region	*Yes*	*No*	*Total*	χ^2
Coastal Andhra	60	180	240	
Telangana	70	200	270	3.30**
Rayalaseema	15	75	90	
Total	**145**	**455**	**600**	

** Not significant.

It is observed from Table 5.62 that the genderwise responses of the hearing impaired students are distributed and Chi-square values were calculated. The obtained Chi-square value is 3.30 which is less than the table value of 6.64 and is not significant at 0.01 level. Therefore, it is assumed that the region of the students does not have any significant effect on their gender wise responses with regard to "the economic utility of the vocational training." Hence, it is asserted that the formulated hypothesis is retained.

The majority of the hearing impaired students from all the three regions (445 out of 600) opined that there was no economic utility with the vocational education courses in which they were undergoing training.

Responses of the Teachers Towards Vocational Education Examination Pattern

To know the responses of the teachers towards vocational education examination pattern, the investigator analysed the collected data with the help of chi-square test and the results obtained are presented in Table 5.63.

Hypothesis

There is no significant difference in the gender wise responses of the hearing impaired students with regard to the "economic utility of the vocational courses".

Table 5.63: Genderwise responses of the hearing impaired students on the "economic utility of the vocational training"

Gender	*Yes*	*No*	*Total*	χ^2
Boys	90	295	385	
Girls	55	160	215	0.255**
Total	**145**	**455**	**600**	

** Not significant.

It is evident from Table 5.63 that the genderwise responses of the Hearing impaired students are distributed and Chi-square values were calculated. The obtained Chi-square value is 0.255 which is less than the table value of 6.64 and is not significant at 0.01 level. Therefore, it is assumed that the region of the students does not have any significant effect on their gender wise responses with regard to the economic utility of the vocational training. Hence, it can be stated that the formulated hypothesis is retained.

From the above table it is clear that the majority of male (295 out of 395) and female (160 out of 215) expressed that there was no economic utility with the present vocational education courses.

Responses of the Teachers Towards Vocational Education Examination Pattern

To know the responses of the teachers towards vocational education examination pattern, the investigator analysed the collected data with the help of chi-square test and the results obtained are presented in Table 5.64.

Hypothesis

There is no significant difference in the responses of the hearing impaired students in relation to management of the school in which they are studying with regard to the "economic utility of vocational courses".

Table 5.64: Responses of the hearing impaired students in relation to management of the school on the "economic utility of vocational courses"

Management	*Yes*	*No*	*Total*	χ^2
Government	50	190	240	
Private	95	265	360	2.131**
Total	**145**	**455**	**600**	

** Not significant.

It is noticed from Table 5.64 that the responses of the hearing impaired students in relation to management of the school are distributed and Chi-square values were calculated. The obtained Chi-square value is 2.131 which is less than the table value of 6.64 and is not significant at 0.01 level. Therefore, it is assumed that the type of management of the school in which students are studying does not have any significant impact on the "economic utility of the vocational training". Hence, it can be stated that the formulated hypothesis is retained.

More number of students studying in government schools (190 out of 240) and private management schools (265 out of 360) opined that there was no economic utility with the present vocational courses in which they were undergoing training.

CHAPTER 6

FINDINGS AND EDUCATIONAL IMPLICATIONS OF VOCATIONAL EDUCATION FOR HEARING IMPARIED CHILDREN

MAJOR FINDINGS

The major findings on the basis of the analysis made of the responses of teachers and students (there is near unanimity in the responses) are as follows:

Teachers

1. Most of the teachers from the coastal Andhra and Telangana expressed that they were not imparting vocational education along with general education. Only teachers from the Rayalaseema spoke in a positive way.
2. Most of the male and female teachers indicated that they were not offering vocational education along with the general education.

3. When compared to the teachers working in government management schools, majority of the teachers working in Private management schools told that they were imparting vocational education along with the general education.

4. Majority of the teachers from all the three regions both male and female and also teachers working in government and private management schools confused that the special schools for deaf were offering vocational education in the following order:

   (i) Tailoring;

   (ii) Book-binding; and

   (iii) Carpentry.

5. The teachers from all the three regions, both male and female irrespective of the management, responded that vocational courses being offered presently in the special schools for the deaf were not useful to take up jobs in future.

6. Most of the teachers from all the three regions, working in government and private management schools and the female teachers favoured computer education for the hearing impaired students, whereas male teachers carpentry.

7. Most of the teachers irrespective of region, gender and type of management responded that the vocational training should be offered from the secondary stage.

8. The teachers from all the three regions, both male and female, working in government and private management schools opined that the vocational training should be introduced from the upper primary level.

9. Most of the teachers irrespective of region, gender and type of management expressed that there was no prescribed curriculum for vocational education.

10. Most of the teachers from all the three regions, both male and female and working in government and private management responded that the aspects related to vocational education were not covered in the curriculum.

11. Irrespective of the region, gender and type of management majority of the teachers revealed that the method of teaching of vocational courses was more theoretical than practical.

12. Most of the male and female teachers from the Coastal Andhra and Telangana, working in government and private management schools indicated that they were not utilising any teaching material to teach vocational education courses whereas the teachers from Rayalaseema region responded that they were using teaching material.

13. Most of the teachers irrespective of region, gender and Type of management pointed out that the time allotted for vocational training was insufficient.

14. Irrespective of region, gender and type of management, majority of the teachers expressed that there was no proper evaluation procedure in vocational training.

15. Irrespective of region, gender and management most of the teachers told that there was no proper evaluation procedure, i.e. neither theory based nor practical based in vocational courses.

16. Majority of the male and female teachers from all the three regions, working in government and private management schools confused that it was better to conduct vocational education examination without confusion.

17. Teachers, irrespective of region, gender and management opined that there should not be minimum pass marks for the promotion of vocational education.

18. Most of the male and female teachers from the three regions, working in government and private management

schools expressed that the certificates were not awarded to students after completion of vocational training.

19. Majority of the teachers irrespective of region, gender and management responded that the vocational education course certificates were not useful to the Hearing Impaired students to put them in an advantageous position

20. Majority of the teachers from the coastal andhra and Telangana regions said that they were not attending vocational training programmes, whereas the teachers from Rayalaseema expressed that they were attending the training programme.

21. Both male and female teachers working in government as well as private management schools responded that they were not attending vocational training programmes.

22. Irrespective of region, gender and management most of the teachers opined that the training programmes in vocational education were useful.

23. Majority of the teachers irrespective of region, gender and management opined that the infrastructure facilities for vocational education were not adequate so as to meet the requirements.

24. Most of the teachers from all the three regions both male and female whether working in government and private management schools expressed that there was a need to have additional requirements such as:

    (i) Funds;

    (ii) Vocational trained teachers;

    (iii) Raw-material;

    (iv) Machinery; and

    (v) Rooms.

25. Majority of the male and female teachers from all the three regions, working in government and private management

schools opined that through providing vocational education, the hearing impaired students would become confident, self-dependent, economically independent and their self-esteem would also be enhanced.

Students

1. Most of the hearing impaired students from the three regions, both boys and girls and from different management schools favoured computer education.
2. Most of the hearing impaired students from all the three regions, both boys and girls, from different management schools expressed that they were undergoing vocational training in Tailoring, Book-binding, T.V./Radio mechanism, Carpentry and Computer etc.
3. Majority of the hearing impaired students irrespective of region, gender and management revealed that the vocational education should be started from 8th class onwards.
4. Most of the hearing impaired students irrespective of Region, Gender and type of management responded that the vocational training should be from the upper-primary level.
5. Majority of the students irrespective of region, gender and type of management expressed that there was no stipulated time for vocational training.
6. Most of the students from all the three regions, boys and girls and from different management schools responded that the method of teaching vocational courses was largely theory method rather than activity method.
7. Majority of the students from the three regions, boys and girls from different management schools responded that there was lack of raw material to learn the vocational courses.

8. Majority of the hearing impaired students irrespective of Region, Gender and type of management said that the availability of rooms for vocational education courses were inadequate.
9. More number of students irrespective of region, gender and the type of management schools pointed out that the availability of machinery for vocational training was inadequate.
10. Most of the students irrespective of region, gender and type of management told that the availability of computers was not in adequate number.
11. Most of the students from the three regions, boys and girls and from different management schools expressed that no vocational education examination was conducted after completion of vocational training.
12. Most of the students irrespective of region, gender and type of management indicated that they were not receiving certificates after the completion of vocational education.
13. Majority of the students irrespective of region, gender and type of management opined that they would like to take up self employment schemes.
14. Majority of the students from all the three regions, boys and girls and from different management schools felt that the vocational education being provided in schools might not help them financially in their future life.

CONCLUSIONS

Based on the above findings, the following conclusions are made:

From the results obtained in the study it is found that the status of vocational education at secondary level for hearing impaired is not appreciable. Not many schools in the state offer vocational education besides general education for the hearing impaired. Only traditional and outdated trades are offered to the children. The method of the vocational education sponsored by the government at the secondary level is to enhance the productivity level of the children.

- The status of vocational component in the schools meant for the Deaf was scanty, ill-equipped and inadequate.
- A very few traditional vocational training programmes were provided in schools such as book-binding, carpentry and tailoring.
- Vocational education component was started in special schools only at secondary level.
- The infrastructural facilities relating to vocational education i.e. accommodation, equipment/machinery raw-materials were ill equipped and inadequate.
- The financial assistance provided for vocational education was nominal.
- The time allotted for practical work was very less compared to theoretical orientation.
- There were no scientifically evolved evaluation/testing procedures in vocational education.
- No certificate was awarded after completion of the course, as a result of it there was a frustration and de-motivation among the students.
- No prescribed vocational curriculum was evolved.
- Fully trained teachers in different trades were a rarity.
- Above all the trades provided in vocational training neither made the students self-sufficient, self-reliant nor empowered the students for self-employment.

EDUCATIONAL IMPLICATIONS

Education is a man making process. The Father of the Nation M.K. Gandhi observed: "Education I mean drawing out the best from child's mind, body and spirit". While developing a system of education to meet the needs of the Indian masses the clearly stated that the system of education should have both immediate and ultimate aims. The immediate aims include 'Bread and Butter aim of Education'. The ultimate aim of education should be 'Self Realization'. ' The Bread and Butter aim of Education' is nothing but the education should make individual as self-reliant. This is the base line philosophy on which the vocationalization of education is seriously considered by the educational planners in the post-independent era. The same is also reiterated by various committees and commissions on education. The vocationalization of education particularly at the secondary level is considered to be utmost important as majority of the students terminate their education at this level and settle in their life. In view of this in-successive plan periods a lot of emphasize has been laid upon the vocationalization of secondary education. But unfortunately the vocationalization of secondary education could not become a successful venture in education due to several reasons which include insufficient resources, insufficient number of qualified teachers and mainly lack of support from the community. Even though, no one can deny the need and importance of vocationalization of secondary education.

If one looks at the scenario of educational facilities made available for children with disability, the situation is very alarming. Though there are a number of provisions to protect the interest of the disabled people in our Constitution, though the national and state governments have launched a number of welfare schemes their position in the mainstream of the society is not as desired. There is an imminent need to expand the educational facility for the disabled at all levels of education.

The vocationalization of education is more pertinent in the case of disabled in view of their specific physical and mental disability. Their survival in the society depends much upon their economic self-sufficiency which is possible only by a way of acquiring certain productive skills. In the absence of that providing general education may not serve the needs of the disabled children.

The educational planners give top priority in providing vocational education to the disabled including the hearing-impaired. To this effect proper budget provisions are to be made in strengthening secondary schools imparting vocational education to the hearing-impaired. Further, exclusive teacher training programmes are to be designed in order to prepare qualified teachers to impart skill based education in the trades where there is demand in the society.

Necessary provisions are to be made in the educational system wherein the students who study the vocational education at secondary level will have access to higher education with flexibility. To conclude that not only creation of educational facilities for the disabled but vocationalization of education from elementary level onwards should be on the national priority, then only it is possible to realize the spirit of the Constitution to have an egalitarian society.

SUGGESTIONS

- The status of vocational education component in the schools for the deaf was scanty and inadequate. There is a need to improve the conditions.
- In additional to the traditional vocational courses provided in schools i.e. Tailoring, Book-binding and Carpentry, New courses which have employment potential such as computer education must be started.
- Vocational training is introduced from the upper primary level instead from the secondary level.
- The infrastructure facilities relating to vocational education i.e. accommodation, equipment/machinery raw materials provided were inadequate, and they need to be strengthened.
- The financial assistance provided for vocational education component was nominal hence, it needs immediate redressed.
- The time allotted for practical work was very less compared to the theoretical orientation and it needs to be rescheduled.

- There was no proper evaluation of vocational component. A systematic assessment procedure with the weightage to practical component is to be planned.
- No certificate was awarded after completion of the courses resulting in frustration and demotivation among the Hearing Impaired. So there is a need for issuing of certificates.
- No minimum pass marks is needed for vocational courses for Hearing Impaired Children.
- No prescribed curriculum for vocational component was evolved. A well designed and systematic curriculum is needed keeping in view the special needs of the hearing impaired.
- Fully trained teachers in different trades are a rarity and hence well trained vocational teachers are to be appointed.
- Above all, the trades provided in vocational courses should necessarily make the students self sufficient, and empower them for self employment.

LIMITATIONS OF THE STUDY

- This study was confined to the vocational education imparting to the Hearing impaired students at secondary level only. Similar study may be conducted at Higher secondary level.
- The present study was confined to the Hearing Impaired students only. Similar study may be extended to other disabled students.
- The present study was limited to limited variables like Region. Gender and type of management. There are other variables like locality, type of school, experience of the teachers etc. that may be considered in the further research studies.
- This study identified the vocational needs of hearing impaired students from the point of view of teacher and students only; it may be extended to the parent's views also.

BIBLIOGRAPHY

BOOKS

Aggarwal, J.C. (2000). *Landmarks in the History of Modern Indian Education*, Delhi: Vikas Publishing House Pvt. Ltd.

Andrew Pollard, June Purvis and Geoffery Walford (1988). *Educational Training and the New Vocationalism*. Philadelphia: Open University Press, Mitton Keynes.

Astuto, T.A. (1982). *Vocational Education Programmes and Services for High school Handicapped Students*. Bloomington: Council of Administrators of Special Education, Indiana University.

Balan, K. (1992). *Education and Employment*. New Delhi: Ashish Publishing House.

Biswa, Ranjan Purkait (1987). *New Education in India*. Ambala Cantt: The Associated Publishers.

Blatt, B., and Morris, R. J. (1984). *Perspectives in Special Education: Personal Orientations*. Glenvew, IL: Scott, Foresman.

Ceeil R. Reynolds and Elaine Flatcher-Janzen (Edrs) (2003) *Encyclopaedia of Special Education*(V0l. 1-3) Newyaler: John wiley and Sons.

James, E. Ysseldyke (1988). *Special Education a Practical Approach for Teachers*. New Delhi: Kanishka Publishers.

Jain Kavita (2004). *Special Education*. New Delhi: Mohit Publications.

Kirk, Samul, A. (1962). *Educating Exceptional Children*. Boston: Houghtom Mifflim Company, U.S.A.

Kirk, S. A. and Gallagher, J.J. (1983) *Educating Exceptional Children* (4th ed). Boston: Houghton Mifflin.

Kokandakar, J.R. (1999). *Aims of Education – A Quest for Rethinking*. Mumbai: Bharatiya Vidya Bhavan.

Lauglo John and Kevin Lillis (2000). *Vocationalisation Education An International Perspective*. Oxford: University of London, Institute of Educational, Pergamon Press.

Moores, D.F. (19780. *Educating the Deaf: Psychology, Principles, and Practices*. Boston: Houghton Mifflin.

Murthy, S.K. (2001) *Philosophical and Sociological Foundations of Education*. Ludhiana: Prakesh Brothers Educational Publisher.

Naik, J.P. (1982). *The Education Commission and After*. Bombay: Allied Publisher Pvt. Ltd.

Ondell, J.T., and Hadin, L. (1981). *Vocational Education Programming for the Handicapped*. Bloomington: Council of Administrators of Special Education, Indiana University.

Panda, K.C. (1999) *Education of Exceptional Children*. New Delhi: Vikas Publishing House.

Quigley, S.P. and Kretsechmer, R.f. (1982). *The Education of Deaf Children: Issues, Theory and Practice*. London; Arnold.

Rao, V.K. (1999). *Vocational Education*. Delhi: Rajat Publications.

Rubin, S.E. and Roessler, R. T. (1983). *Foundation of the Vocational Rehabilitation Process* (2nd ed.). Austin, TX: Pro-ed.

Samuel, L. Odom, Scott, R. Me Connell and Mary, A. McEvoy (ed.) (1992). *Social Competence of Young Children with Disabilities*. Baltimore: Paulh Brookes Publishing Co.

Sharma, P.L. and Jangira, N.K. (1981). *Source Book – Training Teachers of Hearing Impaired*. New Delhi: National Council of Educational Research and Training.

Shankar, Uday (1999). *Exceptional Children*. New Delhi: Enkoy Publications Pvt. Ltd.

Thimmaiah, Seetharamu, Abdul Aziz and Rayappa (1982). Bombay: Himalaya Publishing House.

Venkata Subramaniam, K. (1982). *Issues in Education*. Madras: Macmillan India Ltd.

JOURNALS

Agarwal, Rashmi and Indrakala (1996). Level of Vocational Aspirations of High School Students. Journal of Educational Review. Vol. 11, No.11, November 1996.

Anand, S.P. (2003). Guidance and Counselling for Vocational Education in Schools. *Journal of Indian Education*, Vol. 29, No. 2, Aug. 2003.

Bajaj, K.K. (1998). Vocationalisation – The Challenges Ahead. *University News*. Vol. 33, No. 52. pp.1-4.

Behera, Santosh (1999). Vocational Interests of +2 Girls. *Journal of the Educational Review*. Vol. 105, No. 2, October 1999.

Bhargava, R. (1991). A Study on the Interest and Difficulties Faced by the Students Studying in Vocational Education Stream. Udaipur: State Institute of Educational Research and Training.

Brown, L., Shirago, B., Ford, A., Van Deveter, P., Nishet, S., Loomis, R., and Sweet, A. (1983). Teaching Severely Handicapped Students to Perform Meaningful Work in Nonsheltered Vocational Environments. In L. Brown, A. ford, S. Nisbet, M. Sweet, B. Shirags and R. Loomis (eds.)

Educational Programmes for Severely Handicapped Students (Vol. 13, pp. 1-100). Msfison, WI: Madison Metropolitan School District.

Chandramani, M. and Kalaivani, M. (1993). Survey of Educational Facilities Available for Deaf Children. *Journal of Research Highlights*. Vol. III, January 1993.

Cobb, R.B. and larkin, D. (1985). Assessment and Placement of Handicapped Pupils into Secondary Vocational Education programmes. *Focus on Exceptional Children,* 17(7), 1-14.

Deanna, J. Sands, Lois Adams and Donna, M. Stout (1995). A State Wide Exploration of the Nature and Use of Corriculum in Special Education. *Journal of Exceptional Children,* Vol. 62 (1) 1995.

Dayal, L. Scherich (1996). Job Accommodations in the Work Place for Persons who are Deaf or Hard of Hearing. *Journal of Rehabilitation,* Vol. 62, 1996.

Denetta, L. Dowler and Richard T. Wells (1996). Accommodating Specific Job Functions for People with Hearing Impairments. *Journal of Rehabilitation,* Vol. 62, 1996.

Dhote, A.K. (1991). *On the Spot Study of the Implementation of Vocationalisation of Education Programme in the State of Maharastra,* New Delhi: NCERT.

Emmanuel, M.A.K.J (1970) Vocationalisation of Education at +2 Stage: A Study of Some Major Problems of Vocaitonalisation of Education in Andhra Pradesh. Ph.D. Thesis. Hyderabad: Osmania University.

Faridah Serajul Hag (2003). Career and Employment Opportunities for Women with Disability in Malaysia. *Asia Pacific Disability Rehabilitation Journal.* Vol. 14, No. 1, 2003.

Gogate, S.B. (1987). *A Study of Vocationalisation of Education at Higher Secondary Stage in Andhra Pradesh, Tamil Nadu and West Bengal,* Pan: IIE.

Gokhale. H.V. (1984) *A Study of Vocationalisation at +2 Stage.* Nagapur: G.S. College of Commerce and Economics. Vol. 12(3).

Govinda Rao, L. and Siva Kumar, T.C. (2003). Vocational Training of the Mentally Retorted. Edutraks, Vol. 2, No. 10, June 2003.

Grewel, S.S. and Satish Kumar (1984) Vocational Attitude of High School Students in Relation to Their Intelligence and Adjustment. *Journal Experiments in Education,* Vol. XII, No. 2, April, 1984.

Gupta, V. (1990) A Study of Vocationalsiation of Education at +2 Stage in Uniot Territory of Delhi. Ph.D. Thesis, Bavoda. The Magaraja Sayasi Rao University.

Guru, G., Dhote, A.K. and Ray, S. (1992). *An on the Spot Study of the Implementation of Vocationalisation of Educational Programme in the State of Andhra Pradesh,* New Delhi: NCERT.

James, R. Patton, May E. Crunim and Veda Jairrels (1997). Curriculum Implication of Transition Life Skills Instruction on a Integral Pont of Transition Education. *Journal of Remedial and Special Education,* Vol. 18, September 1997.

Javad, A.K. (1990). A Critical Study of the Vocaitonal Interests of the Students of Arts, Science and Commerce Studying at Post-Graduation Level in Senior Colleges in the Rural Areas. M.Phil. Thesis. Nagapur: Nagapur University.

Jean Whitney, Thomas and Chiryl Hanley – Maxwell (1996). Packing the Parachute: Parent's Experiences on This Children Prepare to Leau High School. *Journal of Exceptional Children,* Vol. 63, No. 1, 1996.

Kathy Wheeler-Scraggs (2002). Assessing the Employment and Independence of People who are Deaf and Low Functioning. *Journal American Annals of Deafness.* Vol. 147. March 2002.

Krishna, Rajneesh and Bihay Kumar Pattnaik (1998). Impact of Education on Occupational Alignments – A Study in an Urban Community. *Journal of Higher Education.* Vol. 21, No. 1, September 1998.

Linda, L. Masino and Robert M. Hodapp (1996). Pareatal Educational Expectations for Adolescent with Disabilities. *Journal of Exceptional Children,* Vol. 62, 1996.

Madan Kundu Alo Dutta, Chrisana Schira, Geist and Lee Crandall (2003). Disability Related Services. Need and Satisfaction of Post-secondary Students. *Journal of Rehabilitation Education,* Vol. 17, No. 2, 2003.

Mary C. Holter and Maria, C. Dinis (2001). Self-Esteem Enhancement in Deaf and Hearing Women Success Stories. *Journal of American Annals of the Deaf.* Vol. 146, No. 4, 2001.

Marhin, A. and Porus, D.C. (1987). Vocational Interests of High School Students. *Journal Experiments in Education.* Vol. 15, No. 7 July 1987.

Mishra, K.M. (1990). Vocational Interests of Secondary School Students in Relation to Their Residence and Socio-Economic Status. *Journal of Educational Psychology.* Vol. 48 (1-2), April, 1990.

Misra, A.K. and Varma, A.P. (1990). *A Quick Appraisal of the Implementation of the Centrally Sponsored Scheme of Vocationalisation of Secondary Education in U.P.* New Delhi: NCERT.

Mohan, S. and Gupta, N. (1990). *Vocational Students' Carrier Behaviour and Their Adjustment in Course at +2 Stage.* New Delhi: NCERT.

Mohanty, G. (1986). *A Survey of Vocational Education in the State of Orissa Since Independence (1974-81).* Ph.D. Thesis. Orissa: Ran University.

Patel, S.P. (1991). *A Study of the Work Experience Programme in Secondary Teacher Training Colleges,* New Delhi: NCERT. p. 78.

Paul, D. Geyer and John G. Schroedel (1998). Early Career Job Satisfaction for Full Time Workers who are Deaf of Hard of Hearing. *Journal of Rehabilitation.* Vol. 64, 1998.

Paul, D. Geyer and John G. Schroldel (1999). Conditions Influencing the Availability of Accommodations for Workers who are Deaf or Hard of Hearing. *The Journal of Rehabilitation* Vol. 1999.

Prasantha Kumar, M.V. (2002). Vocationalisation: An Overview. *University News,* New Delhi: Vol. XXXIX, No. 38 pp. 11-13.

Pandya, Rameshwari (2000). Vocationalisation of Education. *University News*. New Delhi, Vol. 30 (8). No. 3 pp. 4-78 10.

Qureshi, M.N. (2001). National Vocational Qualifications (NVQS) – An Approach Towards Meeting the Global Skill needs. *University News* New Delhi: Vol. XXXIX, No. 8, pp. 12-16.

Raizada, P.L. and Sacheti, A.K. (1990). *A Quick Appraisal of the Implementation of the Centrally Sponsored Scheme of Vocationalisation of Secondary Education in Gujarat*. New Delhi: NCERT.

Reddy, A.V.R. (1984). *Survey of Existing Vocationalisation of School Education Andhra Pradesh – A Report*. Hyderabad: State Council of Educational Research and Training, pp. 33-81.

Resenberg, H., and Tesolowski, D.G. (1982). Assessment of Critical Vocational Behaviour. *Career Development for Exceptional Individuals, 5, 25-37.*

Richard, A., Villa, Jacqueline S. Thousand, Herman Meyers and Ann Nevin (1996). Teacher and Administrator Perceptions of Heterogeneous Education. *Journal of Exceptional Children,* Vol. 64. 1996.

Robert (1989). *A Study of the Socio-Economic Status and Vocational Choice of Students*. M.Phil. Madurai: Madurai Kamaraj University.

Schgd, G.S. (2001). *Work Education,* New Delhi: A.P.H. Publishing Corporation, pp. 1-25.

Sethu Madhava Rao, P.H. (1996). Vocationalisation of Education at the Final Degree Level. University News, New Delhi, Vol. 34, No. 3 pp. 5-7 & 10.

Sundar –Ranjan, S. and Sarch Santhan Kumar, (1993). Teachers Attitudes Towards Vocational Education in the Higher Secondary Schools in Tamil Nadu. *Journal Experiments in Education*, Vol. 21, No. 11. November 1993.

Chunawda, Surga (1987). A Study of Occupational Choices of First Generation Learners. *Journal of Education and Social Changes*. Vol. 1, No. 3, 1987.

Zahn, Suson Brown and Laura J, Kelly (1995) *Changing Attitudes About he Employability of the Deaf and Hard of Hearing*. Journal of American Annals of Deafness, Vol. 140, December 1995.

Swain, B.C. (1992). *Socially Useful Productive Work Experiences Programme at the Secondary State in Himachal Pradesh an Evaluate Study*. Unpublished Ph.D. Thesis. Simla: Himachal Pradesh.

Vanderwodd, MeGrew and Ysseldyke (1998). Why he Cant Say Much About Students with Disabilities During Education Reforms. *Journal of Exceptional Children* Vol. 64, No. 3, 1998.

Varma, B. (1990). *A Quick Appraisal of the Implementation of the Centrally Sponsored Scheme of Vocationalisation of Secondary Education in Delhi*. New Delhi: NCERT.

Easvaradoss, Veena Sumathi, D. and Rekha, B. (2005). Career Decision-making Self-efficacy Among High School Adolescents. *Journal of Psychological Research*, Vol. 49. No. 1, 2005.

Vid, D.K. and Sen Gupta, M. (1990) *A Quick Appraisal of the Implementation of the Centrally Sponsored Scheme of Vocationalisation of Secondary Education in Goa*. New Delhi: NCERT.

Yadav, Raj Kumar (2000). The Vocational Preferences of Adolescents in Relation to Their Intelligence and Achievement. *Journal of Educational Research and Extension*. July-September 2000.

Index

I

J

K

L

M

N

O

P

R

❑❑❑